TABLE OF C

1. A
2. B
3. C
4. D
5. E
6. F
7. G
8. H
9. I
10. J
11. K
12. L
13. M
14. N
15. O
16. P
17. Q-R
18. S
19. T

John Mark Volkots

20. U-V

21. W

22. X-Y-Z

23. Numbers

24. Colors

INTRODUCTION

This book is not meant to teach on dream interpretation, as there are plenty of excellent Christian teachings on dream interpretation by proven and mature people, that I encourage you to read in order to receive a solid understanding and foundation for dream interpretation. I have however provided some helps and guidelines for interpretation in the appendix.

Rather than bring forth material that is already available, my desire instead is to place in your hands over 2400 symbols, with most of them having a multitude or meanings; to assist you and help train you in not only interpreting your dreams, but also the dreams of others.

Dreams are one of the major ways that God speaks to us, therefore it is wisdom to do all we can to understand what He wants us to know through the dreams He is giving us. While it is true not all dreams are from God, when you understand God's language of symbols it become easy to know which ones are from Him or another source. Since it is God's voice we want to understand and know, we are not interested in knowing how the world that is out of touch with God interprets dream symbols. Every interpretation must be God derived; otherwise we will not be receiving truth or what He is attempting to speak into our lives. Therefore, the overwhelming majority of the symbol meanings found in this book are derived from the Bible; with the remainder sourced from tested Christian dream courses, teachers, and interpreting the dreams of Christians.

Any meaning of dream symbols from this or any material on dreams must always be filtered through the Spirit of God. If God is the one speaking to us in dreams, then He must be the final authority on the meaning of any symbols. This book is designed to be an aid, not a crutch to avoid intimacy with Holy Spirit. Holy Spirit should be the first one we turn to for meaning, and using books such as this only as an aid to help us comprehend what He is speaking to us.

Most of the symbols listed have more than one interpretation, therefore it is important to see the meaning in the context of the dream. Some important questions to ask yourself are: what were my emotions or the atmosphere in the dream? Was I fearful, joyful, at peace, angry, etc.? Was it light or dark out? What were the major colors? Was I a participant or an observer?

The context will tell you if the symbol had a positive or negative meaning, and help narrow down the meaning for you. Your own personal life history can also dramatically affect a meaning. As an example if you had a loving dog as a child, it would have a different meaning for you than for a person who was attacked by a dog as a child. Holy Spirit, context, your personal life history and your emotions in the dream are the primary guides to correct interpretation of symbols and the message God is speaking through the dream.

I pray you will enjoy utilizing this book to unlock and understand the messages God is speaking to you through your dream life, and that your life will be wonderfully impacted as a result. I release the wisdom and the mind of Christ and the leading of Holy Spirit to guide you in discovering the mysteries of God in your dream life.

A

Abandoned Car: see automobiles.

Abandoned House: abandoned dreams; abandoned destiny; barrenness; desolation; loneliness.

Abandoned Road: abandoned pathway in life and context will tell if Godly or ungodly life; stubbornness; following your flesh or your own plans.

Abortion: an actual abortion; premature death of a relationship, ministry, plan or destiny.

Acid: something eating at you from within; you are keeping offense towards someone; hatred or malice towards others or hatred and malice towards yourself; burning or destructive words.

Actor: someone pretending to be something they aren't.

Admiral/General: high authority; a major spiritual leader; God.

Adoption: the gift of family; coming into God's family; a desire to adopt; a call to an orphan ministry.

Adulterer/Adulteress: a sure pathway to death of a marriage, spiritual life or ministry.

Adultery: a fear of unfaithfulness; God revealing an unfaithful spouse; pornography; unfaithfulness in the spiritual or natural realm; a pathway to spiritual death; either spiritual or natural adultery is idolatry.

Aging: wisdom; honor; spiritual exhaustion if aging too early.

Aids: a need for compassion on outcasts and the dying; doing something that will lead to irreversible spiritual decline.

Air force: high-ranking spiritual warfare in the heavenlies; protective spiritual covering.

Aircraft Carrier: support during spiritual warfare; a ministry base of operations.

Airplane: operating in the heavenly realms; a personal ministry or church; capable of moving in the Holy Spirit; flowing in high spiritual power; Holy Spirit powered ministry; being taken higher in the spirit realm.

Airplane (Large Commercial): a large corporation or church; a major move of God; flying or piloting a jet liner can indicate employment with a large international ministry or company.

Airplane (Crashing): the end of one phase, or change of direction; death of a high flying ministry.

Airplane (High Altitude): fully powered and flowing in the Holy Spirit.

Airplane (Low Altitude): only partially operative in the Spirit.

Airplane (Soaring): deep in the spirit or moving into deep things of God.

Airplane (Fighter): a call to intercessory ministry or spiritual warfare; high-ranking spiritual warfare from the heavenlies; a fast, disorderly lifestyle filled with parties and drug use.

Airplane (Bomber): spiritual warfare with explosive and impactful weapons.

Airport: a runway is an open pathway for ministry; a large or high powered church that equips and sends out ministries and missionaries; preparing or being ready for launching a ministry;

A to Z Christian Dream Symbols Dictionary

a waiting time in ministry; travel; change.

Alarm: a wake-up call to action; a wake-up call to change what you are doing; a wake-up call to a coming demonic attack; a wake-up call to pray.

Air Balloon: quiet and peaceful rising in the spirit.

Alcohol: being controlled by something or someone other than God; a foolish person; the pathway to destruction.

Alcoholic: pathway to destruction; spirit of addiction; could also mean addicted to wine of Holy Spirit.

Alien: angelic or demonic visitors, context will determine which.

Alligator/Crocodile: a great influencer who influences through strong words or fear; a dangerous person; a lurking danger either in human or spirit realm; a bossy spirit; an evil and large-mouth enemy; like a hippopotamus someone is opening their big mouth with verbal attacks; if they are facing you it means others with big mouths are talking about you.

Almond Blossoms: God's anointing upon a ministry or person; God is about to perform His Word to you.

Almond Tree: God's promise to perform His Word.

Aloe: soothing words; a sacrifice; the sacrifice of Jesus.

Altar: a place of dying to self and laying down your will; a place set apart for spiritual activities which can be good or evil depending on the context; a place of prayer and worship.

Ambulance: emergency spiritual, emotional or physical help; a great need for immediate help.

Ambush: coming attack from a human or demonic enemy; God telling you not to attack or ambush someone.

Amish: not conforming to the world around you.

7

Amphitheater: something someone said or has done is going to be amplified.

Amplifier: a loud and clear message; something said in secret is going to be broadcast to many.

Amusement Park/Fair: carefree fun; amusement; joy in the Holy Spirit.

Anaconda: see snakes.

Anarchy: rebellion; chaos.

Anchor: hope; a steady person or situation; an object or a person to hang on to or to have hope in.

Angel: a messenger; a bearer of good news; a protector; a guardian; a helper; a ministering spirit; good will towards man.

Angry: a hardened heart; foolishness; pride; self-concerned or centered.

Ankles: little faith; early stages of a Christian life.

Animals: talking animals can be demons posing as spirit guides; if they are running on all fours it may mean a powerful person.

Answering Machine: messages or words you need to hear from God or others.

Ant: wisdom; a hardworking attitude; industrious; diligence; an ability to plan ahead or being prepared; being conscious of the seasons of life; an irritation or nuisance; unwanted guests; a harasser; a destroyer; a demonic attack; if crawling all over you, it can mean you have opened some doors to the demonic realm; ant bites can mean little hurts or setbacks; there is something small you need to pay attention to.

Antarctica: feeling isolated; cold emotions; cold spiritually.

Anteater: something or someone out to destroy what others

A to Z Christian Dream Symbols Dictionary

have worked hard to build.

Antenna: a call to pay closer attention to God or His human and spiritual messengers.

Antiques: something old or out dated which can be good or bad; you or someone is hanging onto the past; hanging onto false or useless religious practices or beliefs.

Ape: an overly emotional person; a strong or overbearing person; someone who apes or copies others.

Apocalypse: coming destruction or troublesome times.

Apple: sin; a temptation to do something forbidden; spiritual fruit; something precious; appreciation of others; a time of refreshing; a golden apple can mean wise words; favor; you are the apple of God's eye.

Apple Tree: the love of a husband; a place or situation of temptation.

Apprentice: you are learning a specialized trade; training for particular mission or area of ministry.

Apricot: sharing love and affection with a romantic person.

April Fool's Day: someone is attempting to trick another person; you or another making someone feel or look foolish.

Apron: serving others; miracle prayer cloths.

Aquarium With Fish: a church or ministry; a call to be fishers of men; feeling trapped; feeling others are examining you.

Arab: Middle Eastern or Islamic influence; a call to intercession for Arab people or nations.

Ark (Boat): a refuge; an object of strength; a place of safety during life's storms.

Ark of The Covenant: God's presence, power and glory; a call to intimacy with His presence.

Archaeologist: digging into a matter; hunting for hidden knowledge and revelation; searching to find the good in others; negatively it can mean hunting for dirt in others.

Architect: heavenly wisdom.
Arm: God's power; savior; deliverer; helper; power and strength which can be good or bad depending on the context.

Armadillos: the protective armor of God; a nuisance; a harasser; a destroyer; it can mean someone human or demonic is trying to destroy your emotional or spiritual life.

Armageddon: a major battle or warfare is coming; can mean a call to prayer to counter the enemy.

Arm Band: allegiance; what is written or displayed on the arm band may give insight.

Armor: promised protection by God against attacks; the truth of God's Word.

Armory: bringing stored weapons to bear against the enemy.

Army: a group of believers in unity; an organized group with a cause which can be Godly or evil.

Armored Car: see automobiles.

Army tank: the opposite of a move of God; a corporate move of the enemy in war; if you are going in the same direction it can mean you have major weapons to bear upon the enemy.

Arrow: children; spiritual children; the Word of God; powerful words that can have good or poisonous intentions; poison arrows indicate grief; lies; deceit; curses from the devil.

A to Z Christian Dream Symbols Dictionary

Art: beauty and wisdom of man; what is depicted in the art will give more insight.

Artillery: a battle in your life needs bigger weapons to fight the enemy; if aimed at you it means a human or spiritual enemy is bringing major attacks against you.

Artist: skill; beauty; someone who looks at the good and beauty in others.

Ashes: repentance; mourning; sorrow; pleasant memories destroyed; total ruin or destruction.

Ashen: symbolic of Eastern philosophy, religions or influence; an ashen person means physical or spiritual death.

Asia: Eastern philosophy and beliefs or Eastern religious influence; a call to intercession; a call to missions.

Aspirin: needing or receiving help and relief from a painful situation.

Assassins: witches, satanists or demonic forces with a special mission to kill and steal physically, emotionally and spiritually, or sent to kill a ministry or movement of God.

Assembly Hall: a gathering of people who have similar beliefs and lifestyles; a church or ministry place.

Asteroid: potential destruction to an area of your life or ministry; a potential destructive person.

Astrological Sign: demonic influences; New Age.

Astronaut: visiting heavenly places; seeing other worldly things.

Atheist: refusing to believe God or His Word; one who is unwise and without understanding; an enemy of God.

Athlete: competing in the game of life; a competitive spirit that can be good or bad.

ATM (Machine): mass production; unlimited financial access; God's unending grace and forgiveness; withdrawal against the promises of God.

Atom Bomb: something occurring with great suddenness and power; someone something capable of causing quick and great destruction.

Atrium: having vision; having clear perspective; operating with openness.

Attic: a high place of sacrificial prayer and worship; your mind; the spirit realm; stored or forgotten memories; past life issues; stored up material things we have put behind us; thoughts and ideas we have accumulated and may use again.

Attorney: an intercessor; one who mediates through prayer; Jesus; someone skilled in words.

Auditorium: a place where similar people gather; if gathered with dead people it can mean you have wandered away from truth.

Autograph: prominence or fame; pride; the autograph name may give further insight.

Autumn: transition from one phase and beginning another; a time of completion; a time of change; a time of repentance; a time to harvest souls; a time to reap what you have sown; color and beauty.

Automobile: a ministry; a means of getting to your destination or achieving a goal in life.

Abandoned Car: a stalled or neglected move of God; an unused

A to Z Christian Dream Symbols Dictionary

ministry; a forsaken lifestyle; an abandoned relationship; an abandon project.

Parked Car: ministry on hold; a call to take a sabbatical.

Armored Car: major protection.

Auto Brakes: you need to slow down or stop doing something; stopping an evil or good action; forced to stop something; stopping someone from doing something wrong or evil; a hindrance.

AUTO Brake Failure: lack of self-control; defeat; death.

AUTO Braking Car: a warning to slow down.

Auto Convertible: capable of open heaven or revelatory ministry; a showy or fancy ministry; an easy life; easily able to adapt to a changing situation.

Auto Four-Wheel Drive: a powerful groundbreaking ministry capable of global influence.

Auto Junkyard: a person or a ministry that is abandoned or no longer able to carry out its vision or mission; feeling you have been abandoned or not considered useful.

Auto Rear-View Mirror: looking or focusing on the past; a warning to watch your back.

Auto Seat Belt: needed take action to keep safe physically, emotionally or spiritually; if fastened it means prepared for spiritual warfare; if unfastened it means carelessness or prayer-less-ness.

Auto Tires: indicates the spiritual condition of a ministry,

Auto Flat Tire: need spiritual power, prayer; unable to move quickly in life or go where you want.

Auto Full Tires: a ministry empowered by Holy Spirit.

Auto Bald Tires: not able to see or get a grip on what God has called you to do.

Auto Bumpers: protection.

Auto Air-conditioner: if working correctly it means you are in rest in your situation or ministry; if not working it may indicate you are lax, in denial or have false peace and comfort.

Auto Topless Van: not having adequate anointing for a situation; can mean being vulnerable, transparent and open.

Auto Key: a leader or the one in authority

Auto Van: delivering spiritual goods; a group of people ministering.

Auto Wreck: ministry crashing/falling apart; people clashing, danger; end of one phase before entering the next phase; hindrance in ministry; a hindrance to one's personal destination.

Auto Repair: a ministry to bring emotional, spiritual or physical healing.

Auto (Moving): a move of God; a traveling ministry.
Auto Body Damage: a careless life style.

Avatar: trying to use other people for your benefit; others are trying to use you for their benefit.

Awakening: spiritual awakening; needing to be alert; needing to be watchful and ready for action or for the next move of God.
Axe: the end of a thing or season in your life; pruning useless and sinful things in your life; issues that need to be settled.
Battle Axe: the Word of God.

Dull Axe: a situation that needs wisdom; dull in wisdom; you are working hard but little is being accomplished.

B

Baboon: acting poorly in social settings; aggressive person.

Baby/s: spiritual infants; birthing a new work; new ideas; beginning to be productive; something in its infancy or early stages; innocence; dependence; helpless; a gift from God.

Baby Stroller: expecting a new thing to come; expecting an actual baby.

Baby food: if eaten in a dream it means you have need for the meat of the Word.

Back: someone has your back for protection; something pertaining to your past; someone turning their back on you; someone ignoring or dismissing you; something concealed or out of view.

Back door: if someone is entering through the door it can mean a secret or sneak attack.

Backhoe: a major change or renovation; someone digging into or exposing your past.

Back Porch: history; looking at things in the past which can good or bad.

Backpack: life situations or weight on a person's back slowing them down; can mean provisions for travel; provisions for a traveling ministry.

Backside: something in the past or behind you; something or

15

someone concealed from view or understanding; someone out to blind side you.

Backsliding: losing physical, emotional or spiritual progress.

Backstage: something or someone behind the scenes or hidden which can be good or bad depending on the context; something or someone waiting to be revealed; you are about to be noticed or recognized; your ministry is about to be seen and recognized.

Bacteria: a root or cause of a problem; a small problem or situation that can cause major upheaval or destruction.

Bad Breath: being self-conscious; using poor choice of words; a bearer of unpleasant words or news.

Badge: a symbol of authority or honor.

Badger: someone is pestering or bothering you; you are pestering or bothering someone.

Bag: a journey; provision for a journey or ministry; what's in the bag will tell you more.

Baggage: can be things you are carrying from the past or from a past relationship; sin in your life; God wants you to move forward in life or ministry; can also mean much provision for a major move in ministry.

Bagpipes: talk that has no value or understanding; no credibility; no anointing.

Bait: something or someone intending to lure you into a trap.

Baking/Bakery: producing or preparing something for work or ministry; God's provision for you or your ministry; preparation for a welfare ministry.

Baker: an originator; one who serves; a visionary.

A to Z Christian Dream Symbols Dictionary

Balances: something reflecting both sides of a matter, which can tilt one way or the other in your favor; judgment; trying to keep emotionally stable during stress.

Balancing: needing order in your life; wavering; being indecisive.

Balcony: overlooking or overseeing people, a project or a ministry; being at a vantage point to see the whole picture of a situation.

Balding Head: being spiritually uncovered; not having adequate prayer or protection; lacking wisdom.

Bald Tires: see automobiles or tires.

Ball: someone's sphere of influence; if you have the ball it can mean you are in control of an area or sphere of influence; if another has the ball it can mean you are under their authority or control of an area of influence.

Ballroom: having joy and fun in life.

Ball Gown: prepared for something that requires elegance or grace.

Balm: healing; anointing; someone is relieving pains, stress or agony in another's life.

Banana: good fruit in one's life.

Band: collaboration and teamwork.

Band-Aid: trying to fix a big problem with small or insufficient resources.

Bandage: a time of healing and recovery; needing to cover an emotional or spiritual wound with prayer to bring healing.

Bandits: a group of demons coming to raid you.

Bank: a heavenly account; God's favor for a future season; a place of safety and security; God's provision for now and in the future.

Banker: an accountant or money manager; an angel; Holy Spirit.

Bankrupt: spiritual or emotional exhaustion; feeling you are a failure; feeling depressed and oppressed.

Banner/Flag: victory and rejoicing in Christ; a ministry covering which you are committed to; someone who brings unity, love, or purpose; a unifying object or circumstance.

Banquet: the love of Jesus; God's affirmation in the presence of our enemies; God's provision; a full cup; much affluence and abundance; satisfaction; blessing; celebration; structured teaching of the Word of God.

Baptism: moving from the natural to the spiritual; dying to self; expression of the new man.

Baptizing Yourself: trying to earn salvation or favor with God.

Bar: an atmosphere of sinfulness; you may be surrounded by sinful people and demonic spirits.

Barbarian: not understandable.

Barbecue: being satisfied with your spiritual life.

Barbed Wire: someone or something stopping or hindering you; someone or something keeping you from your destiny or ministry.

Barbershop: a period of changing beliefs, customs or habits; a church where change can take place; a place of vanity; a place of correction; removing or needing to remove old covenants of religion, sin, or the occult.

Bare Feet: humility, depending on the context it can also be lack of peace; vulnerability; pain.

A to Z Christian Dream Symbols Dictionary

Barking: a warning; a spirit or person trying to intimidate you.

Barrenness: unproductive; a difficult time or period in your life.

Barn: God's storehouse of provision for you; blessings; stored spiritual wealth; a dependable place of security and safety; a church.

Barrel: being over a barrel means you are helpless against someone's power.

Barricade: someone or something protecting you from sin or wrong action; someone or something stopping you from receiving what is needed.

Baseball: competing in the game of life; pay attention to running bases and sliding home.

Basement: to be abased; humility; unseen part of something; storage zone; something or being hidden; our soul; our carnal nature; being discouraged; feeling depressed; a refuge; a secret sin; can also mean confinement; a prison; your foundation if the basement is below ground level; if cracked it means weakness in foundations of faith, problems in a person, church or business; look for activity of anyone to see if they hidden and what they're doing; can mean someone with a secret motive or agenda is working behind the scenes for either good or bad; if they're killing snakes it is good; if waiting to sneak up to attack it is bad; something below the surface is going on either for good or bad.

Basket: God's provision; delivery of provision; prosperity if it has good fruit; can mean escape; can mean a measure of judgment.

Basketball: the game of life; if the other team is taller it can mean a difficult spiritual struggle; if you are ahead and playing well it means you are doing well spiritually.

Bat: an unclean demonic distraction; witchcraft; a human satanic instrument; a person of darkness.

Bathing: cleansing from sin for holiness; what you doing on the outside to prevent an unclean or unholy attitude; outward repentance.

Bathrooms: a need to clean out sin in your life; God is cleansing you of sin, bad habits or addictions; a time of confession and repentance; a place of transparency and facing reality in your life; a place of desire; a place of passion; strong lust.

Battery: limited spiritual power and energy.

Battering Ram: you are engaged in spiritual battle; if used against you it means a person or a demon is trying to break you down.

Battle: every battle is God's to win; spiritual warfare; intercession.

Battleship: a call to intercede to defeat a large future attack; major spiritual weapons.

Bazooka/Machine Gun Aimed at You: a major spiritual attack; can mean you're to call an intercessor to pray for you; if you are aiming the gun it indicates you are being called to intercession or heavy warfare.

Beach: if looking at the water it means you are waiting for someone or something to take place or happen; if walking or sunbathing it means you are at peace; can also mean waiting for Jesus to come.

Beam: power or illumination coming from God or the heavenlies; a time of exposure or being in the spotlight.

Bears: the fear of the Lord; reverence; respect; danger; a wicked person; a wicked spirit; vindictiveness; something or someone

A to Z Christian Dream Symbols Dictionary

evil; someone or something that is after something you possess; an unexpected and fierce attack; someone who appears calm but is very explosive or volatile; if you're the bear it can mean you may become very volatile over an issue; context will reveal it is good or bad.

Beard: having respect for authority; not operating in your right mind if the beard is messy; operating with the mind of Christ if trimmed.

Beaten: a demonic attack; correction for foolish action; the sacrifice of Jesus.

Beating Someone Up to Get Them to Listen to You: you are forcing something on someone or forcibly trying to get them to do something. If you are being beaten it means someone is forcing something on you.

Beauty Shop: a place and time of preparation; emphasis on outward appearance or self; vanity.

Beaver: a diligent worker; negatively it can mean you or another is trying to dam up the river of God from flowing in your life.

Bed: needing emotional rest and healing; the marriage bed; a refuge; contentment; intimacy; a place of revelation; laziness or being lax.

Bedroom: a private place; a place of peace; a place of intimacy; a place of covenant; a place of revelation; a place of prayer; a place of self-made conditions.

Beer: can indicate bickering and fighting; addiction.

Bees: swarming enemies; stinging words; gossip; busybodies; being more noisy than effective; a double edged situation capable of going bad; able to produce sweetness or pain; a demonic attack.

Beetles: a problem that is hard to overcome.

Begging: under a curse.

Behead/ Head Injury: rebellion against authority or the head.

Belching: speaking evil; speaking curses.

Bells: announcing something; a call to holiness; a call to pay attention; a call to action; bringing alertness; a public warning; speaking something loudly.

Belly: appetites and lusts; worldly desires; feelings; spiritual well-being; Holy Spirit river.

Belt: truth; the whole truth and nothing but the truth.

Bestiality: a spirit of perversion.

Bible: a call to study God's Word; a call to be obedient to God's Word; the final authority.

Bicycle: your movement through life; personal ministry; a move of God in one's life; a ministry dependent on much human effort; if the bike has broken parts or missing wheels it can mean problems or troubles with the person who owns or is riding the bike.

Big Butt: laziness or apathy; butting into other people's business without being invited.

Bigfoot: a large problem in your life, a major problem person; someone has their big foot on you holding you down in life or spiritually.

Billboard: a sign or warning marker; something God or someone is get you to notice about your life, what was on the billboard is the message.

Binoculars: looking ahead; looking into the future; looking beyond your present situation; prophetic ministry.

A to Z Christian Dream Symbols Dictionary

Biohazard: a warning of something deadly in your life.

Birds: a messenger; a symbol of a leader either good or evil at different levels; Holy Spirit or an evil spirit depending on if the color is white or black.

Blue Bird: revelation is coming your way; order; obedience.
Eagle: a symbol of personality; you are capable of soaring in the Spirit; having good focus; swiftness; powerful; a prophet of God.

Owl: an evil eye that watches; a spirit of craftiness; able to see in spiritual darkness; ability to hear.

Robin: obedient to God; a sign of a spring time in your life; a fresh life or beginning is coming.

Woodpecker: a nuisance; someone who pecks away at you with words.

Sparrow: the Father's watchful care and your value to Him; God's desire to provide.

Stork: following God's commands; doing what one is supposed to do; a new ministry, experience or opportunity; actual pregnancy or baby.

Mocking Bird: someone is or is trying to mock or scorn you.

Black Crows: someone is or is trying to harass you.

Dove: Holy Spirit; peace; a seal of approval from Heaven.

Vulture: an evil spirit; an opportunistic person; someone who preys on human weakness.

Raven: a sign of an unclean spirit.

Cardinal: seeing cardinals is a sign that God wants you to know something very important.

Feathers: a protective covering; a shield or instrument for flying or moving in the spirit.

Wings: a protective covering or a shield to someone; flying or moving in the Spirit; a place of refuge and safety; God's presence; being provided a way of escape from danger.

Birth control pills: controlling your own life instead of letting God rule.

Birth/Labor: announcing or bringing forth a new thing; multiple births mean a series or a multitude of new things; if born as a toddler or teenager it the new thing in your life has not yet reached maturity; born old, or with missing teeth or gray hair means you are not able to maintain the energy of a new thing in your life.

Birthday Cake: celebration of your life and spiritual growth; if the cake is half-baked or burnt it can mean worthlessness.

Birthday Presents: coming gifts from God; spiritual gifts.

Biting: if biting or being bitten it means strife and quarreling; backbiting; a human or demonic attack; consequences of alcohol.

Bitterness: symbolic of sin and an evil heart.

Black Belt: spiritual warfare; expertise in prayer.

Black Cat: often means witchcraft.

Black Horse: can mean spiritual famine.

Black Panther: an evil, cunning or sneaky person; a predator coming after someone.

Black Sheep: an outcast; unwanted; undesirable actions that result in rejection.

Black Widow Spider: a demonic attack; a woman who devours men.

Blanket: spiritual covering or protection; a love for others.

Blast Furnace: God's fire doing a fast and heated work in you; a hard life; worldly living.

Bleach: cleansing; purity.

Bleeding: suffering; if a nose bleeds it can mean strife or quarrels; an emotionally hurting person; losing spirituality; verbal accusation; a traumatic experience.

Blemish: sin; perceived flaws.

Blind: lack of understanding; ignorance; not able to see into the spirit world.

Blindfold: something or someone blocking you from truth or revelation.

Blind Spot: not able to see your own faults; not able to see problems coming.

Blizzard: a blindness to a situation; resistance to your spiritual growth.

Blood: life itself; a curse if the blood is on the ground; atonement; having to appease someone.; something that testifies.

Bloody: killing; death; deep emotional or spiritual wounding; feeling emotionally or spiritually beat up.

Bloody Water: war; troubles; woes.

Blood Transfusion: being born again; being revived or given new life over a situation; being rescued

Blossoms: coming fruit in someone's life.

Blueprints: strategy or plans for someone's life or situation; God's strategy for a ministry.

Bluffing: can mean you are not thinking things through; you are taking a blind chance instead of faith based on truth.

Blushing: embarrassment; shame.

Boa Constrictor: see snakes.

Boar: a devourer; a curse upon you, your family or property.

Boat/Ship: a place of testing if you are in a storm; if you are stepping out of the boat it means faith; usually stands for a personal or a church ministry.

Battleship: a ministry built for effective spiritual warfare.

Crashing Ship: an end of ministry or end of one phase.

Fast Ship: operating in great Holy Spirit power.

Large Ship: a large church or ministry capable of large areas of influence.

Shipwreck: a disaster in life; a loss of a ministry or position.

On Dry Ground: ministering without the power of Holy Spirit; works of the flesh.

Sinking Ship: being out of line with God's purpose; losing spiritual control; sinking of a ministry or one's own faith; trouble upon you or coming upon you; impending disaster or failure in your life; failure of a larger work or ministry.

Small Boat/Ship: a small or personal ministry.

Multiple Ships: a group or organization with many on board; large ministries.

A to Z Christian Dream Symbols Dictionary

Boat (Sail): Holy Spirit powered ministry; a ministry free or highly mobile; freedom to go where Holy Spirit takes you.

Cruise Ship: an easy position in life; if sinking it means disaster or troubles in life.

Schooner: speed on water indicates you will breeze through your circumstance or into your destiny; able to influence people.
Body: symbolizes the flesh; an emaciated body can mean sin in a person's life.

Body Armor: a protected person.

Body Builder: a wise person; symbolic of moral and physical strength; can also mean someone is trying to intimidate you.

Body Guard: a spiritual mentor; a friend; a protector.

Body Odor: a call to take better care of yourself either physically, emotionally or spiritually; an unclean spirit trying to attach itself to you and your life; the after effects of fleshly or sinful action.

Bogyman: a demonic oppressor.

Boiling Water: someone is in trouble; evil poured out on someone; someone trying to get you in hot water or you trying to get someone in hot water.
Boils: judgment; testing; suffering.

Bombs: Holy Spirit power; negatively it can mean anger; someone or something that will cause major problems or damage to you or to a ministry.

Bones: substance of something; the main issue; something long lasting; if it's a skeleton it can be something without substance or details; spiritual death; feeling hopelessness.

Broken Bones: a broken or crushed spirit; a contrite heart; grief; envy.

Book: learning; gaining understanding or knowledge; a time of preparation; the Bible; revelation; a promise from God; the title of the book may be the message or revelation.

Book of Life: an invitation to receive Jesus as Savior; an invitation for intimacy with God; secure in God.

Boomerang: words or actions that will come back upon you which can be good or bad depending on the context.

Boot: see shoes.

Boot Camp: preparation and training for ministry, intercession and spiritual warfare.

Boss: an authority figure; a parent; a teacher; a pastor; supervisor; leader.

Bottle: your body as the container of anointing; a need to keep information bottled up or secret.

Bows/Arrows: bitter words; being prepared for war; the source of physical, emotional or spiritual attacks; the power of a person or nation; an arrow means a verbal attack; if the bow is bent it means you are ready for war; if it is in the hands of another it means they are ready to make war against you; God's weapons against the enemy.

Bowing: submission; you are burdened with heavy loads or the cares of life; can also stand for an idol in your life.

Bowl: you are measuring someone or something up; provision; what is in bowl will give more insight.

Boxer: hostile or intimidating person; a person who brings fight-

A to Z Christian Dream Symbols Dictionary

ing and dissention.

Boy Scout: helping or serving others.

Bracelet: pertaining to pride; something valuable but of the world; it may mean your identity or another's identity if it has a name on it other than yours.

Brakes: see automobiles.

Branches: God's people; churches; a church split; if cut down and burned it can mean what you have been doing is not useful or God inspired.

Branded: having something etched in your mind or spirit; marked out as belonging to God your mind or spirit is closed off.

Branding Iron: being a slave or addicted to something.

Brass: strength; hardness of heart; a hard covering; judgment; something has you captive; something hard to break away from.

Brazen Face: not having any fear; not fearing God; a hardened person.

Bread: Jesus the bread of life; the Word of God; a source of nourishment; God's provision; money; the body of Jesus.

Fresh Bread: a new word from God.

Moldy bread: something that is not new.

Unleavened bread: purity showing a lack of sin.

Bread and Butter: something that will bring you income or spiritual prosperity.

Breast: a source of milk for new believers; a source of spiritual sustenance; an ability to nurse young believers; enticement and seduction.

Breastplate: God's protective shield; you or someone being protective of vital issues or concerns.

Breath: the spirit of man; the breath of life; Holy Spirit; a sign of spiritual life; receiving a fresh start in life.

Breathing Fire: hateful and destructive words.

Bribery: coercing or enticing someone to join go along with you; wickedness against someone.

Bricks: building people up with strength; slavery and bondage to sin or a habit; something man made; a ministry or something designed to last; a strong personality.

Bride: the bride or church of Jesus Christ; a covenant relationship; a natural marriage.

Bridal Shower: finding love; celebrating love; being celebrated.

Bridegroom: Jesus Christ; an actual bridegroom.

Bridge: you are crossing over to a new place in life or ministry; someone or something will take you across an obstacle; a connection between two people or circumstances; someone or something that holds you up in difficult times.

Bridle: a curse; stubbornness; having control over someone or a circumstance; self-control; controlling or a need to control your tongue; a law, leader or government controlling for either good or bad.

Briefcase: business you need to take care of; the corporate world; plans for a ministry or mission.

Briers: a prickly person; something wild and thorny in your life that needs to be trimmed away; someone or something uncultivated or false; someone or something that needs to be avoided.

Bright (From Light Source): God's light in your life; a revelation; the end of the tunnel or solution for your situation; God's presence.

A to Z Christian Dream Symbols Dictionary

Brimstone: the judgment of God; punishment; a time of testing.

Broken: a loss of spiritual power, authority or influence.

Broken Arms: powerlessness

Broken Pot: crushed by sin; can mean someone who has died physically, emotionally or spiritually because of grief in life.

Broken Window: a demonic opening into your soul; your peace or joy is being stolen by a spiritual thief; an inability to see in the spirit or having a distorted spiritual view.

Bronze: strength; fortitude.

Bronze Gate: imprisonment; protection; if opened it can mean an invitation to ministry to a particular person, group or nation.

Bronze Wall: strength; protection; negatively it can mean a major hindrance.

Brook: a provision of God; someone or something that brings refreshment; wisdom; prosperity from God; if the water is dirty it can mean you are contaminated by sin or an ungodly influence.

Broom: cleaning your life of sin; if it's a broomstick it means witchcraft; evil curses.

Brother/S: can be literal; a dear friend; Jesus or an angel; the body of Christ; a Christian brother or sister.

Brother-in-law: same as brother, but under special obligation; a spiritual brother without true love; a person of another church who is also a believer; an actual brother-in-law or someone with similar qualities.
Brownies: love; fellowship; family; spiritual food.

Bruise: affliction; a result of battling the enemy; a bruising event or circumstance that leaves one with hurt feelings in need of healing; the suffering of Jesus on our behalf.

31

Brush/Comb: caring for your spiritual covering.

Bucket: being useful for service; provision or supplies for your life or ministry; God is giving you a measure of peace, rest, power or authority.

Bubble Gum: if it is stuck on you it can mean a tricky or sticky situation; if blowing bubbles it can mean immaturity or not taking life seriously.

Buccaneer: a hard driving and argumentative person.

Buck (Deer): a lover, fiancé or husband.

Bucket: if flowing with water it means prosperity and life in the spirit.

Buckler: protection.

Buddha: means someone who is filled with Buddhist influences.

Buffet: life choices.

Bugs/Insects: destruction; ruin; a pesky or meddlesome person.

Bug Bites: misfortune; irritating actions from others.

Builder: a person of wisdom; a person who builds other people up.

Buildings: can mean spiritual places you frequent; the spiritual or emotional condition of a person, place, church or church office; the size or height of the building can give more insight as to whether it is speaking about an individual, a company or a ministry.

1st floor: the natural or physical realm where we live under heaven.

2nd floor: 2nd heaven where angels war fueled by our prayer; the demonic realm.

A to Z Christian Dream Symbols Dictionary

3rd floor: the 3rd heaven, where we visit with God in paradise.

Bull: a threatening person or situation; warfare may be coming; a strong enemy coming against you; can also be economic gain coming.

Bulldog: a stubborn person; a determined or tenacious person.

Bulldozer: someone who bulldozes their way into your life; someone who overpowers others to get their way; clearing ground in your life; tearing things down either good or bad.

Bullets: words or information used during gossip and slander.

Bulletproof Vest: a well-armed Christian; being well protected against emotional or spiritual attacks.

Bullfrog: demons and unclean spirits.

Bum: being bummed out over a situation; feeling unwanted or an outcast; a wandering person; can mean a demon oppressor being cast out.

Bumper Sticker: a position you agree with; a message you spread or advertise.

Bundle: a measure of harvest; fullness; action gathered for reward or judgment.

Bunny: for non-believers it means luck; fertility and magical power; it can mean multiplying pests in your life; the realm of the demonic.

Burden: can be a person's sin or anxieties in life; can also mean carrying other people's problems.

Bureaucrat: a difficult and inflexible person.

Burglar/Robber/Thief: satan; a thieving spirit, a human or demonic enemy trying to steal your peace, joy or rest in the Lord.

Burial: a permanent end of something or a situation.

Buried Alive: sudden helplessness.

Burn/s: consumed over something; heated up or angry over someone or something; a sign of fervency or being stirred up in the Spirit; burning spiritual fleshly desires; financial oppression.

Burning Bush: announces a supernatural commissioning; a sign; God wanting your attention.

Burning Coals: cleansing; kindness.

Burned Out: the enemy has either ravaged or will try to ravage you in the future.

Bus (Moving): a large move of God in a ministry; working together; a teaching ministry if it is a school bus; the ride of life for a non-believer.

Bus Boy: serving others in a lowly fashion.

Bus Station: you may be waiting for departure or start of a ministry; a center for ministry or deliverance; you may be ready to move on in life.

Bush: can mean a person's growth; a call to ministry; you may be trying to hide from truth or responsibility if you are hiding behind the bush.

Butler: a trusted person in a position of service.

Butter: encouragement; someone who brings soothing words or comfort; someone using smooth words that can be good or bad depending on context.

Butterfly: a change is coming in your life; going from one glory to another; beauty; a socially adept person.

Buttons or Zipper on Mouth: keeping quiet; a need to keep

A to Z Christian Dream Symbols Dictionary

quiet.

Buzzard: an unclean or impure person; a demonic spirit; some-one trying to ravage or pick you apart.

Buy: trying to acquire something in the natural or spiritual realm which can be good or bad; trying to buy or earn favor with God or others.

C

Cab or Taxi: a temporary mode or time in your life journey; a temporary ministry; being carried along in your life or ministry.

Cabin: a need for seclusion; a need for intimacy; a need for quiet or peace.

Cactus: a prickly person or a prickly situation; a hindrance in life; someone with a sharp or prickly tongue.

Caddie: a trusted advisor; carrying someone's load or burdens.

Cage: feeling or being trapped in a situation; feeling restricted; being limited or held captive; feeling everyone's eyes are on you; a call to guard or watch.

Cafeteria: spiritual food; a place or time of spiritual nourishment; serving; a teaching ministry; a ministry of helps.

Cake: provision from heaven; celebrating a person's life; if half-baked or burnt it can mean worthlessness.

Calculator: counting the costs of something.

Calendar: timing of a promised thing; timing of ministry; seasons of one's life; waiting for a specific day or event to occur.

Calf: a situation or ministry that is set to increase and grow; a young ministry with lots of energy.

Camel/s: coming provision; God is making it possible to go through a door that is impossible without His help; having a

A to Z Christian Dream Symbols Dictionary

servants heart; able to bear other people's burdens; an intercessor's heart.

Camera: memories in life either good or bad depending on the context; capturing a moment; if another is taking your picture it means your life is the focus.

Camouflage/Fatigues: being hidden in Christ; feeling unnoticed; able to blend in situation without notice or fanfare.

Camp or Campgrounds: something temporary in your life; passing through a situation or time of life; temporary provision.

Cancer: something emotionally or spiritually deadly is eating at you that can spread or get worse if not dealt with.

Candle: your life; the Word of God; your impact or influence in others or in a situation; if not lit it can mean a lack of God's presence.

Candlestick: someone who carries the light of God; the Spirit of God; the church.

Candy: immaturity if it is the main diet in the dream; a lure or temptation.

Cannibalism: injustice; an evil person or spirit; oppression of the poor; someone or something is trying to devour your natural or spiritual life or goods.

Cannon: a major spiritual weapon that can be good or bad depending on if you are the target or if it is pointed at the enemy.

Capital Building: rule; authority; government.

Captain: the one in charge; the Lord; a pastor.

Cars: see automobiles.

Carpenter: Jesus the Builder of your life; one who makes or amends things or situations; a preacher, an evangelist or a laborer in the harvest.

Carried: need rescuing or carrying; if you are being carried it means protection, shepherding or covering by God or the person carrying you.

Cartel: an organized group of spiritual enemies.

Cartoon: silliness or immature behavior in an adult.

Casino: you are gambling at life; worldly living; winning is symbolic of worldly treasures.

Casket/Coffin: an actual death; spiritually dead; death to a dream or desire; a call to prayer.

Castle: a stronghold either good or bad.

Cat: a cunning or sneaky person; a predator; someone coming after others; a deceptive situation or person; an unclean spirit; craftiness; a witch or witchcraft waiting to attack; a habit that could be dangerous; an actual personal pet.

Catapult: can mean you will be launched very quickly in ministry; going forward quickly in life or through a situation.

Caterpillar: a season of hiddenness before transformation; a devouring curse or demonic spirit.

Cathedral: old religion or beliefs; a religious spirit in operation.

Catholicism: religious traditions; a religious spirit in operation.

Cattle Prod: wise sayings; the Word of God; God or another attempting to move you to action.

Caution Sign: a warning to proceed slowly in a situation or with a person.

Cave: a place of escape; a refuge and safe hiding place; a secret place of encountering God; a place of darkness in your life.

Cave Man: a rude or brutish person; a secretive person; feeling lonely or a lonely person; a secretive life.

Cedar Tree: a strong or flourishing person or ministry.

Celebrity: a desire to interact with famous or important people; a desire to become famous.

Cell Phone: can mean God trying to reach you; can mean you are addicted to your phone and connection with the world; incessantly ringing can mean being overly talkative or overly busy.

Cemetery: death of a dream or a desire; feeling spiritually dead.

Censer: prayer; a call to prayer.

Certificate: a feeling of accomplishment; being given authority to do something.

Chaff: a wicked or worthless person.

Chains: can represent addictions, imprisonment or bondage; to be bound in the spirit can be bad or good depending on context; being bound to God; being bound in sinful, unhealthy or unpleasant situations or circumstances.

Chair: authority over something or someone; coming into position of authority; the throne of God.

Chameleon: you are able to blend in; you are someone who likes frequent change.

Champagne: victory; a cause for celebration; trying to find joy apart from God.

Championship Belt: God's protection; a champion in God's army.

Change Dream Because You Don't Like the Way it is Going: the Lord is telling you to change things in your life so something bad doesn't happen or to make something good happen.

Channel: a way out or a situation; a process of time; a difficult time leading to the next stage; being kept on course.

Chariot: a place in God; a coming encounter or life destiny; a vehicle for spiritual war.

Chase/Being Chased: a time to flee; a time to get rid of something in your life; a call to pursue or go after something; being pursued by a physical or spiritual enemy; if being chased by a legitimate authority figures it means you are not being submissive to authorities over your life.

Chasing the Wind: stupidity; folly; worthless action or tasks; chasing dreams or positions not meant for you.

Cheating: if cheating at a game it means you are using unethical or underhanded tactics in your life; adultery.

Check: a seal of a promise; a guaranteed promise; wages in a person's life; unexpected income.

Checkmate: assured victory in a situation.

Cheerleader: a positive and uplifting person; the God Head.

Cheek: can be a vulnerable part or time in your life; you are returning love for anger when people hurt you; beauty.

Cheetah: an unclean spirit; a speedy outcome in a situation; an agile and fast moving ministry.

Cheese: to comfort or soothe.

Chef: great at serving others; a call to feed others spiritually.

Chess: being locked in a strategic battle with people or the demonic realm.

Chicken: fear or cowardice; an evangelist; gifting; a caring spirit; a gathering or mothering spirit.

Chief: being in charge; leadership or authority.

A to Z Christian Dream Symbols Dictionary

Childhood Home: influence from the distant past that can be good or bad depending on the context.

Children: something new that you are going birth; birthing new ideas or a ministry; a prophetic ministry; God's blessing, joy and peace; your natural children; the next generation.

Chimney: smoke from a chimney means something will quickly disappear in your life.

China: can be a call to minister in China; Eastern religious beliefs in you or others; a call to pray for China.

Chisel: something man-made; something permanently etched in a person's heart or mind.

Chocolate: can be fleshly desires; addiction to fleshly things.

Choking: biting off more than you can chew too fast or too much in the wrong way; if choking another person it can mean hatred for them; if you are being choked it can be the worries of the world; if watching others being choked it can be a call to intercede for them against a spiritual or human attack.

Christmas/Tree: a new thing in Christ; tradition of men; spiritual gifts; a season of gifts or love; a time of joy and reaching out in love to others.

Christmas Wreath Over a Mantle: something may happen at Christmas time; a season of time; can represent a time frame in your life that you need to deal with.

Church Building: a person's religious activities or beliefs.

Cigarette: addictive or negative behavior.

Cinderella: feeling used or disrespected by other; future hope coming.

Cinnamon: a holy anointing; you are pleasing and set apart for God.

Circle (Ring or Round): a circumstance that is endless; signifies an agreement or covenant; if you are making a circle it is relating to the universe; walking in circles means you are in a spiritual wilderness or you have lost your way spiritually.

Circumcision: a call to cut off things of the flesh; coming into liberty; covenanting with God; a blood relationship: going to new levels in your spiritual walk; being born again.

Circus: a busy atmosphere; a confusing atmosphere or situation; you are treating life like a circus.

City/Cities: a busy and bustling life; if filled with happy people it means righteous; if high on a hill it means blessings; if being torn down it means wickedness; circumstances in our lives; the makeup of a person; all that has been put into a person; a group of people; a church; God's inner city work; the character or what a specific city is known for.

City (Dark): stands for satan's influence over a person or an area where they live.

City (Golden): Zion; the city of God.

City of Jerusalem: physical or spiritual inheritance in your life coming from that direction; can mean you have Jewish blood; a call to pray for Jerusalem.

Civil War: fighting or arguing with friends or family.

Clapping: the joy of the lord; a sign of approval or celebration of a person.

A to Z Christian Dream Symbols Dictionary

Classroom: a time of spiritual preparation; a person with a gifting to teach others.

Clay: a delicate and fragile situation; not feeling secure; the frailty of man; the human body; a believer.

Climbing: moving up in life, on a job or ministry position; trying to get a better position in life; going spiritually higher.

Cloak: something hidden or mysterious; a mantle of anointing or authority.

Clock: a situation where timing is very important; a time to do something that was revealed to you; an actual time may refer to Bible passages; you are running out of time to do something; God is telling you that it is a time of waiting; there is an issue that depends on God's timing.

Close: to shut up or be silent; to be hedged or walled up which can be good or bad.

Closet: a secret place; something hidden; a confidential situation; something that is personal; exclusive; wanting a place of prayer and intimacy with God; negatively can mean others are secretly plotting against you or a ministry.

Clothing: a covering either pure or impure; your standing or authority in a situation; a mantle; your calling or what you are going to be doing.

Swim Suit: you are in the flow of Holy Spirit.

Speedo suit: Holy Spirit will do or is doing a fast work in or through you.

Cultural Clothes: a call to a nation.

Tearing Clothes: repentance; grief or sorrow.

White Clothes: you are the righteousness of Christ.

Dirty Clothes: sin; dead works.

Clouds: a heavenly manifestation; the glory of God's presence.

Hurricanes or Tornadoes: are they dark or light? It could be that God is coming to destroy everything so you can get to where you are going; someone or demonic enemy want to destroy you.

Dark Clouds: a dark or stormy time in your life; being fearful; possible trouble from an natural or demonic enemy.

White Clouds: the Glory of God; something coming from God.

Rain Cloud: God's presence; God's favor; Holy Spirit anointing.

Rain Cloud with No Rain: someone claiming anointing and gifting that does not exist.

Clown: happiness and joy; a person who is not serious about life; someone not taking God seriously; acting or being childish; a human or demon heckler.

Club: your spiritual instrument of war against the enemy; God destroying your enemies.

Coal: kindness; God's cleansing and purification; the fire of God's love.

Coast Water): looking for Christ.

Coat: spiritual covering; endorsement; if multicolored its high favor with humility; a protective covering from an attack; righteousness if clean, and the opposite if unclean or dirty; cultural clothing may be countries or areas you may be ministering or a call to intercede for them.

A to Z Christian Dream Symbols Dictionary

Coattail: being connected with another's success; feeling left out or left behind by others.

Cobra: see snakes.

Cockroach: demonic spirits; coming trouble if you allow little sins or bad actions and habits to remain in your life.

Coffee: a need for awakening.

Coffin: person dying physically, mentally, emotionally or spiritually; can mean someone coming out of spiritual death into new life in Christ.

Cog: you are a small but crucial part of a movement or an organization.

Coins: stewardship; financial issues; if two coins it can mean poverty or debt, or an orphan lifestyle or mentality.

Cold Drink: refreshing or good news.

College: learning great or high truths in God's Word; learning greater lessons of life; high promotion in the spirit or physical realm.

Columns: foundations or leaders that people put trust in; can be a spirit of control and manipulation.

Coma: being out of touch with reality in life; a feeling of detachment from others or life; your true hidden nature.

Comforter: Holy Spirit; a friend in time of need.

Communion: unity within the Body of Christ or family; communion or intimacy with God.

Compass: your life direction; a direction God wants you to go in your life.

Complaining: being ungrateful, unthankful; a rebellious person.

Computer: information; you are wasting your time on the unimportant.

Conceive/Conception: birthing something new; adding or multiplying; a process of preparation.

Concentration Camp: an oppressive place or situation; an emotional or spiritual prison; under demonic oppression.

Congregation: a local church body; bringing people or something together; an appointed meeting.

Construction worker: building or edifying oneself or others; building a ministry.

Controlled Flying: your spiritual maturity is increasing; you are trying to control your spiritual growth.

Convertible: see automobiles.

Conveyer belt: a production line of many things or whatever is shown; being taken in a direction outside of your will and control.

Cooking: preparing spiritual food.

Convict: a dangerous enemy either human or demonic.

Cop: an earthly or spiritual authority.

Coral: high value; beauty.

Cord: something or someone holding things together; adding strength to another person, ministry or situation; unity.

Corn: a multiplication of a spiritual harvest; spiritual food; a seed of healing; yellow corn can also mean fear or hope depending on the context.

Corner: you are about to turn the corner in a situation; an unexpected circumstance in life that will cause you to change directions suddenly.

Cornered: being put in a compromising position of helplessness.

Corner of House: living with an argumentative person.

Cornucopia (Horn of Plenty): a time to be thankful; a thankful person; pretending you are someone you are not.

Corpse: spiritual death and judgment; you are dead to your flesh, old sins and habits.

Costume: someone playing a role or pretending to be someone they are not.

Couch: rest and relaxation; at peace with another if sitting with them; at rest in God; if the couch is colorful it can mean an adulterous woman.

Counsel: the path to victory; wisdom for life.

Counselor: Holy Spirit; Jesus; a true friend.

Counterfeit Money: false teaching or doctrine.

Country Side: feeling isolated; a time of peace and tranquility; a restful situation; an unexplored potential.

Court: being held accountable for your actions; judging the actions of others which can be good or evil.

Courthouse: a time of judgment; a time of persecution; a trial time or being on trial in a situation; coming justice in a situation; a call to prayer to avoid a potential miscarriage of justice.

Covered wagon: powerful tradition that is good or bad depending on context; can mean pioneering a ministry depending on context of the dream.

Covering: protection; shield; security; authority; loving others; covering or protecting others.

Cow/s: spiritual food and a source of enrichment; a gluttonous woman or wife; an oppressive situation or weighty burden; a wealthy women living in ease or luxury.

Cowboy: a loner; someone who is self-sufficient or has an independent spirit.

Crane (Bird): mindless chatter.

Crane (Machine): involved in a major project or ministry; building up someone's life.

Craps (Dice Game): taking chances in life or in a situation.

Crawling: someone being sneaky; cowering in shame; humility or are being humiliated; a new believer.

Creation: a period of great creativity coming your way.

Creditor: can be a curse on someone's life.

Crocodile: something or someone dangerous; an old lurking spiritual enemy; someone with a big mouth; see alligator.

Crooked: something is being distorted; someone not being straight or truthful; someone distorting the truth.

Crooked Mouth: perverse or wicked speech; someone not being truthful.

Crops: a coming time to harvest or plant; provision or coming provision; something to do with time and fulfillment.

Cross: death; a call to die to self; Christ's crucifixion; if the cross is on an animal it means false religious belief or demonic doctrine; if the cross is colored pay attention to the color for further meaning.

Cross Dresser: someone not living in their true identity; someone oppressed and influenced by spirit of perversion.

Crossing Street: changing perspective; changing a place of operation; changing sides.

A to Z Christian Dream Symbols Dictionary

Crossroads: a vital choice must be made; a necessary change in life direction, position or belief.

Crowd: masses of people around the world; can mean a compromise of your values; you are allowing things or worry of the world crowd out faith or God.

Crowing: bragging; pride; a denial of Christ.

Crown: a symbol of authority and power; royalty; Jesus Christ our Lord and King; reigning in life or in a situation; going to be honored or rewarded; if the crown is made of thorns it means mockery and persecution.

Crucifix: Christ's death before resurrection.

Crushed: being or feeling overwhelmed by a situation or a person; can also stand for sin in one's life.

Crutches: vices; coping mechanisms; addictions.

Crying: needy or needing help; a period of grief, sorrow or mourning; intense emotional expression over a situation which can be good or bad depending on the situation.

Crystal: value; beauty; a fragile situation or relationship; a clear understanding about a situation or relationship.

Crystal ball: divination or sorcery.

Cub: playfulness; caring; can also be symbolic of fierce anger.

Cultural Clothes: a call to a nation; a call to intercede for a nation.

Cup: partaking or participating in a situation; your portion in life; God's provision; shared beliefs or activities; being used by God.

Cursing: worthlessness; wickedness.

Curtain: concealment; being secretive; hiding from life or reality.

Custodian: a position of trust; a caretaker.

Cymbals: time to praise God; negatively it can mean without genuine love for yourself or others.

Cypress Tree: a symbol of God.

D

Dam: a blockage or barrier to flowing in the Spirit; the power of unity; gathering resources; reserve sustenance or provision; stillness; uncovering hidden earthly or spiritual treasures.

Dancing: celebration; joy; God's grace; help in times of trouble; a time of rejoicing; can be a time of worshipping God or an idol; can mean a wild lifestyle.

Dangerous Situation: if you are trying to scream, but nothing or only a whisper comes out it means you are in a major spiritual battle and the enemy is trying to keep you from growing in the things of the Spirit; you can't scream because circumstances, people or the demonic realm are working in your life to choke off your passion for prayer and God is telling you that you need to pray more.

Dark Path: an evil place; you are going down a path to sin; you have lost your way.

Darkness: feeling or being surrounded by evil; absence of God's light.

Darts: you are on target for a goal; you are aiming at a goal or something in particular; if the darts are piercing, penetrating, or painful, it means you are being attacked or will be attacked in the natural or spiritual realm, therefore it is a call to prayer to ward off the attacks.

Date (Fruit): beauty; love.

Date (Romantic): a love interest in your life either in the physical or spiritual realm.

Daughter: uniqueness; a gift of God; a ministry that is your child in the spirit; an actual daughter or one with same qualities.

Dawn: loving kindness; a new day coming in your life; a new opportunity coming.

Daytime: an opportune time; a time of light; a season of good deeds; a season when matters are revealed or understanding is gained.

Darkness: dark dreams are demonic, but are also an opportunity for prayer to defeat the enemy's plans.

Deacon: honor; dignity; trustworthiness; a servant.

Dead Body: one who has been attacked by satan; a need for a spiritual awakening; one dead spiritually or not operating in the gifts of the Spirit; death to a dream, desire or ministry.

Deadwood: spiritual death; unwanted weight to a situation or a ministry, someone who is a continual heavy burden to others or a ministry.

Deaf: not spiritually attentive or paying attention to God's voice; not being attentive to another person or a situation.

Death: may be a warning of impending physical death; can be a person's need for spiritual awakening; may be a demonic attack; a need to die to self in an area; needing a separation from evil habits or sin; it almost always means we go from death to life in the spirit realm.

Death Row: inescapable correction or punishment; inescapable death to a relationship or a ministry.

Debt: an outstanding obligation owed.

Debt Collector: a curse upon someone's life.

A to Z Christian Dream Symbols Dictionary

Debtor: a foolish person; foolish behavior.

Decoy: a snare; lure; bait; a trap.

Deep Water: can mean you are in over your head in a situation; you are in a spiritual river.

Deer: incredible ability to take great strides in life or other areas; sure-footedness in situations; a spiritual longing for God and the things of God; a symbol of peace; a symbol of longing; youth and beauty.

Deer Blind: someone lying in wait to harm another.

Delivered from Pigs: delivered from demonic activity that was very destructive and messy.

Demon: an evil spirit; a call to prayer to defeat the enemy in yourself or others..

Den: busy doing the wrong or useless activities.

Dentist: a need for or getting help with your choice of words; a need for or getting help in understanding God's Word.

Deodorant: covering up offensiveness.

Department Store: symbolic of life choices.

Depression: being oppressed in life or ministry.

Desert: a place of isolation and insulation from the world; being cursed; feeling or being spiritually dry; barrenness, a place of lack; a place of relying on God; a place of testing.

Desk: a place to conduct business; an official office in the church; a symbol of authority; a time and place of learning.

Despair: a loss of hope; a need for God to intervene in a situation.

Detective: you are searching out a matter or situation in your life.

Devil: threatening demonic activity.

Dew: spiritual or natural blessings; the Word of God; being watered by God.

Diamonds: a hard or hardened heart; a person that cuts with hard words; beauty; value; strength, may represent an April birthstone.

Diaper: if soiled it means sin; an immature person or ministry; a person who is always making messes that others have to clean up.

Died suddenly: a sudden encounter is coming that is going to be life changing; going from spiritual death to spiritual life; death to sin and the garbage in your life; dying to self.

Dieting: being self-conscious; desire to lose physical or spiritual weight; removing the weight of sin, addictions & worldly interests in your life.

Dice: you are taking risks or gambling with your or another's life.

Dictator: a domineering person; can stand for your boss, spouse or pastor.

Difficultly Walking: a difficult times of life; facing opposition.

Digging: hard labor for that which is hidden; can mean you are judging others for either good or bad; you are digging into the life of others for either good or bad.

Dimes: tenfold or ten times over.

Dining Room: eating spiritual food; feeding on the Word of God; the table of the Lord.

A to Z Christian Dream Symbols Dictionary

Dinosaur: something is outdated or disappearing in your life; there is something big and terrible from your past but God has dealt with it; things planted in your life that have been forgotten but when uncovered at a later time will be valuable.

Diploma: recognition of completion or mastery; you have passed a test of life; authorization; maturity.

Directions (North, South, East, West): a place or interest to pray over; a move in life either physically or spiritually..

Dirty Clothes: false doctrine; impure spiritual things; sin; dead works; a spiritual condition in need of attention.

Discipline: someone willing to receive correction means being wise; someone fighting against discipline and/or talking back to authority means being foolish.

Disease/Infirmity: a literal sickness; sin; emotional problems; bondage of the enemy.

Dishes (Dirty): sin; hypocrisy.

Dishes (Clean): holy and righteous living.

Disney World: a time to rejoice and enjoy life and the Lord; it can mean you are living in a pretend world, being fearful to live in reality.

Disqualified: someone who refuses to follow the rules or submit to legitimate authority; a rebellious person.

Ditch: a place of supply or provision; a deterrent; a place of being stuck; a place of deception; a trap; fleshly desires that lead to problems or sin; preparation for flowing in the Holy Spirit.

Diving: falling or diving headlong into danger; diving headlong into a ministry or project.

Divorce: division, disillusionment or disconnection from

55

people or situations.

Disk Jockey: someone who brings joy and happiness to others.

Doctor: the Great Physician; Jesus; a healing anointing; someone with a caring ministry; a minister; if you are the doctor it stands for your authority or expertise in a situation in life or in another's life.

Doe: a young wife; can be a reference to finances.

Dog: loyal friend; a gift that can be harnessed to do good but should not be trusted too much; something that could be versatile in function but unpredictable; can mean being ungrateful; worldly or evil people; can be fears about being attacked by actual dogs or demons; may mean you are worried about the health of your pet.

Dog (Growling): can be demonic sentries to guard sinful or evil things in your life to keep you in bondage.

Dog (Bites): an attack by an evil spirit; someone attacking you with their mouth.

Dog (Ear): pulling a dog's ear indicates you are meddling in other people's business, or they are meddling in your business.

Dogfight: a fierce spiritual or human attack.

Chihuahua Dog: a person or friend that is talking all the time; a person who gossips.

Bulldog/Pitbull: tenacity that can be bad or good; fierceness and savagery in conversation and action.

Yappy Dog: someone always opening their mouth in gossip; an un-wise person.

Dominos: can be symbolic of being the cause of a series of good or bad events.

Donkey: a stubborn person; stupidity; a person God can use if surrendered to Him.

Door: a new opportunity; a hindrance in an area of your life if the door is locked or blocked; if an animal or person is blocking the door it means it is a spiritual hindrance; a door can also indicate a free spirited person; it can also symbolize a person's mouth; it can mean walking through a situation; walking into a new area, new opportunity or a new ministry; Jesus the way.

Doorway: a person waiting at an open door can indicate the pursuit of wisdom or pursuit of God.

Double Image (of Yourself): a demon has assumed your image in a dream to bring fear; it can also mean your personal angel depending on the context.

Double Edged Sword: the Word of God; negatively it someone who is speaking out of both sides of their mouth.

Double Number: double of what the number stands for.

Dove: Holy Spirit; peace; rest; gentleness; anointing; a young woman.

Down (Direction): spiritual descent or backsliding; falling away; humiliation; failure

Downward Spiral: you are on a path leading to physical or spiritual death; you are moving in the wrong direction in life.

Drag Race: someone who lives an out of control, foolish and fast paced lifestyle; a reckless person.

Dragon: satan; a high ranking demonic spirit; someone at a great level of wickedness; an antichrist spirit.

Drain: you are discarding something worthless.

Dripping Faucet (Tub or Sink): indicates disagreements and arguments; a complaining or critical person.

Driving (Fast): person who is in a hurry in life; a reckless person.

Driving (Reckless): carelessness in life.

Driving (Slow): cautious and careful; negatively it means fearful in life and not living in the rest of God.

Drawing: an ability to conceptualize things; an ability to express yourself; being fluent in expression, doctrine, truth or deception.

Dreadlocks: rebellion; if dreadlocks are in the hair with a colorful towel they think they are doing something for the Lord, but are actually acting in rebellion; dreadlocks originate from Eastern religion that says we are Gods and can do what we want, with the ability to take young people to nurse them from weakness to strength; this type of dream is an early Jezebel category.

Dreaming in a Dream: a deeply spiritual message; a futuristic message; it is extremely important because it often has to do with destiny, life calls, or things God does not want you to miss.

Dreams From Daily Life: all soulish are not bad because it means God is cleansing us from things that have built up in our lifetime; the context can tell you what He is doing.

Drinking: receiving from the spiritual realm which can be good or bad depending on the context; receiving your portion in life; bearing your cross; an addiction to alcohol.

Dripping faucet: disagreements or arguments; you are a constant irritation to someone or someone is a continual irritation to you.

Driving: one in charge of a ministry or leading a move of God; the one in charge who makes the decisions.

Driving Backward: losing progress or backsliding; not going in the correct direction that corresponds to your anointing.

A to Z Christian Dream Symbols Dictionary

Drought: a time of lack; dryness with God.

Dross: wicked people; sin in your life.

Drowning: sorrow; grief; overwhelmed by a situation leading to depression; overwhelmed to the point of self-pity; an attack from people or the demonic realm.

Drugs: if illegal drugs it's a sign of addiction; can mean a counterfeit anointing; can represent healing either physically, emotionally or spiritually if prescription drugs.

Drums: a unifying force in battle or worship.

Drunk: being influenced by a counterfeit source of anointing; self-indulgence; selfishness; rebellious; addiction or uncontrolled lust.

Dry Ground: ruin or apathy to spiritual things; recognition of a need for God and spiritual water.

Duck: a noisy or boisterous person; a person who is too talkative; having an uncontrolled mouth.

Dumpster: something needs to be removed from your life; if you are the dumpster it means you have too much garbage in your life or are living a worthless lifestyle.

Dung: something unclean or worthless in your life that needs to be discarded.

Dungeon: represents being a prisoner of the demonic realm or a person; being a prisoner of a lifestyle, habit or addiction.

Dunk: dunking a ball in a game symbolizes power, skill and gifting.

Dust: inactivity; neglect; lack of use; death; something in your life has died; atrophy; old flesh; temporary nature of humanity;

frailty of man; a curse; it could mean God wants you to dust off something you let go of or put on a shelf.

Dust Devil: symbolic of small or manageable troubles.

Dying: symbolic of physical or spiritual death; death to a habit or addiction; death to a situation; death to self.

Dynamite (Explosion): a major danger; an explosive person or situation; a coming emotional explosion; great spiritual power that is either good or bad; Holy Spirit power.

E

Eagle: see birds.

Ears: being attentive; listening; symbolic of a prophet; hearing spiritual things that either build up or tear down; a lack of hearing; a need to pay more attention.

Earmuffs: spiritual deafness; rebellion and refusing to hear.

Earring: wisdom or wise counsel; can also be reproof; seduction or alluring; being a slave to someone or something.

Earthquake: a shaking of your life foundation or belief; a sudden release of great spiritual power; coming ground shaking changes; a great shock or trauma in your life; a time of trial; release from an emotional or spiritual prison; a time of trouble or judgment.

East: God's glory; judgment can come out of the East.

East Wind: knowledge of man; useless talk; judgment.

Easy Chair: authority over a family or organization; power within an organization; feeling comfortable in your situation or life.

Eating: consuming spiritual food or truths from God; meditation and gaining greater understanding; feeding on evil or the lies of the enemy.

Eavesdropping: a busybody.

Echo: the Word of God coming back; repercussions or reaping what you have sown for either good or bad.

Eclipse: judgment; end time events.

Edge: being on the edge of a building or cliff means a desperate or dangerous situation where you need God's help and peace; on the edge of a breakthrough.

Egg: incubation time ; a time or waiting; a delicate situation; a seed or promise; a possibility for growth, potential and development in any manner; sustenance and provision; a time of revelation; incubating wealth; wealth acquired unjustly if the egg is taken from you.

Egypt: slavery and bondage; pre-Christian life; worldly living.

Eighteen Wheeler Truck: blessing or judgment of a ministry; a large ministry capable of carrying or supporting many outreaches; a major care ministry.

Elderly Person: wisdom and understanding.

Electricity: the Spiritual power of God; a potential for God to flow through you.

Electrical Outlet: the possibility of being connected into Holy Spirit's flow; if the cord is plugged in it means you are connected to Holy Spirit's flow and power; if the cord is unplugged it indicates you are not connected to Holy Spirit's power.

Elementary school: learning the primary essentials; not yet mature; infant stage.

Elephant: a large un-dealt-with sin or major problem or situation that cannot be concealed; wisdom and strength; someone with big ears listening to gossip.

Elevated: high social status; favor in life; a high ministry position.

Elevator: implies travel between the natural and spiritual

A to Z Christian Dream Symbols Dictionary

realms; can be rapid advancement or rapid fall depending if you are going up or down; moving up or down in levels of Godly authority; like stairs, they mean transition, only faster; can mean faster promotion in the spiritual or secular realm or faster demotion if going down; the number of the floor you stop on may tell you whether it is good or bad; a rapid change in anointing.

Elves: helper angel assigned to help you in life or ministry; negatively is means demonic spirits.

Emeralds: royalty; may be a time line for the month of May.

Emotions: emotions in your dreams usually are literal feelings you are experiencing.

Employee/Servants: one who is submitted to authority; the actual person.

Employer/Master: Jesus; an authority figure either good or bad; a pastor; evil leadership.

Empty House: feeling abandoned or lonely in life.

Engine: great power; can stand for anointing; can be something critical or what is powering or fueling a person's life or situation either good or bad.

Entangled: you are unable to get out of a situation; a time or place of trouble; in distress; in bondage to sin, habit or addiction; in an ungodly affair.

Envy: jealousy with a vengeance; revealing covetousness in one's life.

Eraser: getting rid of sin, bad habits or addictions; erasing guilt and condemnations of past mistakes and bad decisions in life; God's cleansing and forgiveness of sin.

Escape: fleeing from danger or a call to flee from temptation.

Eunuch: able to dedicate yourself to a cause.

Evangelism: a call to evangelism; a wise person.

Evening Gown: your calling requires elegance and grace.

Ex (Spouse or Love): may reveal lingering emotions that need healing from past relationships.

Exam/Tests: a coming test in life; a call to prayer for coming tests.

Exercise: increasing spiritual strength; exercising godliness.

Executioner: you are having to carry out unpleasant tasks or orders from other people.

Exile: action designed to cleanse you of wrong behavior.

Exit Sign: your way out of sin, trouble, temptation or addictions.

Exorcism: a need for deliverance; your spiritual authority over the demonic.

Explosion: a sudden emotional outburst; a sudden expansion or increase coming; a quick work or change coming; negatively can be a devastating change; an explosive situation or person.

Exterminator: one who helps take care of problems in your life or in the life of others.

Extra Innings: symbolic of high pressure and intense competition during an event in life.

Eyes: prophetic vision; a seer anointing; being watchful in prayer; being watchful for temptations of the eye or lustful temptations;

Eyes (Large): an ability to see everything or the whole picture in a situation.

Eyes Closed: ignorance; spiritual blindness that is mostly self-imposed.

Eyes Winking: concealed intentions; a cunning or devious person.

Eye Shadow: arousal; sensuality.

Eye Tooth: vision or revelation.

Eyewash: cleansing your spiritual eyes to see from God's viewpoint; being a hypocrite.

F

Face: symbolic of humanity; identity or characteristics of a person; a way of expressing your feelings.

Face (Dark): demonic.

Face (Light): angelic.

Faceless Person: usually means the Holy Spirit; angels often come to us and are usually just out of our sight.

Face (Pale): death or anguish.

Face (Smiling): joy and peace.

Face (Without Eyes, Ears, Mouth): being deaf and dumb to the truth or the gospel.

Factory: a feeling of monotony in life; a place in life that is routine; structured service in God's vineyard; being productive; accomplishment.

Fainting: a lack of spiritual or emotional strength.

Fair (Carnival): a time or place in life of fun and enjoyment.

Fairy: a hovering familiar spirit; a life of fantasy.

Fall (Autumn): a time of change or a new thing coming in your life; a time to reap what you have sown; a time of reward and harvest.

Falling: feeling a loss of control in life or a situation in life; seeing someone else fall may be a call to pray for them; can be a sign

A to Z Christian Dream Symbols Dictionary

of not having Godly guidance; feeling a loss of support; falling out of favor with someone; entering a time of trial; feeling in spiritual darkness; sin.

Falling and Waking Up: waking up to where your life has been headed.

Family: your actual family; your spiritual family; group of people in covenant or a spirit of oneness; unified fellowship; an attempt to draw attention to your relationship with your family; if a relative is deceased in your dream it could mean a generational curse or blessing that comes from that relative; if they are dripping oil or are radiant and joyous it indicates eternal life.

Family Pictures: family historical issues which can be good or bad depending on the context and who is in the pictures and your relationship with them.

Famine: misfortune; loss; lost hope; lost intimacy or closeness with God.

Fan: stirring up gifting; something or someone who brings relief or comfort; someone or something stirring things up either good or bad depending on the context.

Fangs: lies; wickedness; danger; someone may be trying to suck the life out of you.

Farm: a place of provision.

Farmer: one who plants, nurtures and cares for new believers or others; a laborer; a minister, preacher or pastor capable of or is presently sowing and reaping a harvest; Jesus Christ.

Farming: wisdom and plenty; providing spiritual sustenance for others.

Farsighted: you cannot see things at hand or what is right in front of you; an ability to see the potential or future outcome of

67

an action, idea r ministry.

Fast/Quick: an easy task; quick results.

Fat: if eating fat in a dream it may indicate you are taking things that belong to God; you are eating the wrong spiritual food.

Fat Cat: a rich person; rich in the wrong things; pride.

Fate: vanity and death.

Father: an authority figure; God; an originator; the source of something; an inheritance; a tradition; a provider of needs; a supplier of identity; father of the bloodline; the head of a home, place or organization; an actual father.

Father-in-Law: father figure in an organization; advisor; head of another organization, spirit of delegation.

Fatigues: God's army; ready to battle the enemy.

Fawn: youth; beauty; vitality; future adventure or possible accomplishment.

Fear: nightmares or fearful dreams are almost always demonic; anxieties in life; drug use both illegal or prescription; can be a warning dream from God that is either a call to prayer or to have you change a course of action or lifestyle..

Feast: a time of plenty, happiness, fun, enjoyment and good times.

Feather/Pinions: a protective spiritual covering; something with which to move into the spiritual realm; the presence of God, Holy Spirit or angels; comfort; evidence of angelic protection and presence in your life; depending on the circumstance it can be confusion; depending on the context a person or creature with feathers in a dream can also be an evil spirit.

Feeding: to partake in spiritual provision either good or evil; involved in or a call to be involved in a care ministry.

A to Z Christian Dream Symbols Dictionary

Feet: your life journey; a spiritual walk; your heart attitude.

Barefoot: humble before the presence of God or others.

Diseased Feet: a spirit of offense.

Kicking Feet: not under authority or working against authority.

Lame Feet: crippled with unbelief; a negative stronghold.

Overgrown Nails: a lack of care about your spiritual life; a life or walk not in proper order.

Washing Feet: humility.

Dirty Feet: walking in sin or heading that way.

No Feet: symbolic of trusting in a fool; living foolishly.

Fence: marks spiritual territory; protection; security; self-imposed protection; a limitation; a stronghold that can be overcome; can also mean a person under pressure.

Fence (Barbwire): a dangerous obstacle or situation in life.

Ferris Wheel: doing the same things over and over without getting anywhere.

Ferry: an event carrying you to your destination or destiny.

Festering Wound: unconfessed sin; can also be emotional injuries or pain caused by another.

Festival: joy; thanksgiving; fellowship with other believers or people of like mindedness.

Fever: fighting off spiritual or demonic infection; a sinful lifestyle.

Field: a life ready for new things; ready for spiritual growth; a life situation; things to do and accomplish.

69

Field (Empty): unused portion of your life.
Field (Ready for Harvest): upcoming harvest in your life; maturity; a call to evangelism.

Field Goal Kicker: a high pressure situation in which you or another person plays a critical role in determining the outcome.
Fig Cake: a call to intercession; revival.

Fig: love; goodness.

Fig Tree: upcoming honor if the tree is healthy; if unhealthy it can mean being unproductive; may be a sign to get rid of something in your life that is not bearing fruit..

Fight/Fighting: spiritual warfare or struggles in one's faith; resisting someone or something; if you are fighting relatives it indicates shame and disgrace; if fighting other people it indicates bitterness and anger towards them.

Filing Cabinet/Files: a collection of memories, events or situations; negatively it can mean you are storing past wrongs done to you.

Finger: a means of discernment; spiritual sensitivity; feelings; an ability to relate; direction; able to intertwine with others; creativity.

Clenched Finger: pride.
Finger of God: the work of God; the authority and power of God.

Index Finger: a prophet.

Middle Finger: an evangelist.

Pointed Finger: accusations; persecutions; instructions; direction.

Small Finger: a pastor.

Thumb: an apostle.

A to Z Christian Dream Symbols Dictionary

Finger Nails: spiritual weapons; if painted can mean seduction.

Fire: a raging problem in one's life; God's presence; trials or persecution; a burning fervency for God or something good or bad depending on the context; a strong emotion; a strong longing; an aching to do or see something; a deep craving; deep anger; judgment; punishment; destruction; a roaring fire is usually God devouring the enemy; Holy Spirit fire burning away the junk in us; continual pure worship that is tested.

Fire Alarm: a warning of impending trouble or of a heated situation.

Fire Breathing: a vicious and scathing verbal attack.

Fire extinguisher: extinguishing trouble; a call to put out heated arguments or disagreements.

Firefighter: a person who helps extinguish problems between people; one who helps out in times of trouble.

Fish/Fishing: evangelism; a call to be a fishers of men; the newly recreated spirit of man; miraculous provision of spiritual or physical food.

Fish Hook: being hooked or caught that can be bad or good depending on the context.

Fish Net: signifies a large catch or large success.

Fish Tail: a car fishtailing means losing control in life.

Fist: aggression; anger; rage.

Flag: an emblem of a specific nation or group of people may be a call to prayer or a call to missions to that nation; can also be a symbol of God's love and protection.

Flame Thrower: burning & highly destructive words.

Flamingo: instruments that carry out the purposes of God.

Flash (Light): sudden revelation or insight.

Flat Tire: see automobiles.

Flea: inconvenience; a minor problem or person that causes irritation; a subtle problem

Fleece: testing; faith; approval.

Fleeing: being pursued by an enemy; demonic torment; God chasing your enemies.

Flesh: earthly desires.

Flies: rottenness; ruin; a demonic attack.

Flight: swiftness or easy progress in life.

Floating: to rise above one's problems.

Flock: can mean great property and wealth.

Flood: troubles in life; being flooded with an enemy attack; a major demonic attack that will see God come to your aid or rescue; judgment on those who use power to inflict violence on others; sin judged; being overcome and unable to recover; troubles; grief.

Floor: being on the floor means humility or humiliation; the ground floor of a new ministry, project or company.

Flowers: man's glory of the flesh that is passing away; an offering; the glory of God; a beautiful expression of love; a time of renewal; it can mean Springtime which indicates springing forward; Jesus lily of the valley; love, courtship and romance if a rose; the fragrance of one's life which can be good or bad depending on the fragrance and color; a budding or blossoming relationship or situation.

Flushing Toilet: ridding oneself of a sin or a situation; getting rid of something worthless..

A to Z Christian Dream Symbols Dictionary

Flute: joy; celebration; praise and worship; can also mean sorrow depending on context.

Fly: ruin; rottenness; evil spirits; an evil person or situation; corruption; possessed or controlled by an evil spirit; the results of unclean actions.

Flying: swift progress; highly Holy Spirit powered; flying like an eagle indicates high spiritual activity that God is taking you to; high spiritual growth or advancement is coming; overcoming life's burdens; escaping bad situations; little resistance; total control in a situation.

Flying With an Angel: a greater spiritual issue.

Flying Serpent: a deadly or hard to kill persistent enemy.

Flying on Fire: the fire of the Lord is on you; the power of the Lord is on you; you will be purging spiritual issues from people you come in contact with.

Flying Near Power Lines: flirting with danger; imprudence; foolish actions.

Fog: a situation of short duration; something not clear to you; a short time of uncertainty; a time you are concealed; something is hidden or vague to you.

Folded Hands: inaction or sluggishness.

Food: spiritual and physical nourishment that can be bad or good.

Fool's Gold: a counterfeit relationship or religion.

Foot: you are on a journey.

Foot (Broken): can mean faithlessness.

Foot (Cut Off or Missing) trusting in a foolish person.

Foot Print: following someone else's path in life; if the foot print is bloody it means the path of wrongdoers.

Foot Stool: worshipping God; an enemy is subject to you.

Fork: ability to feed oneself or another spiritually.

Form of an Animal: if you can see through them it means it is demonic and a spiritual issue.

Foreigner: a non-believer; someone to be taught and cared for and brought into God's family; someone or something not of God; someone operating in the flesh; a demonic being.

Forehead: the human thought process and reasoning; revelation; an ability to retain and recall spiritual truths; a commitment to God; renewing your mind; the peace of God.

Foreskin: unrepentant sin and rebellion; being legalistic.

Forest: an isolated or dangerous place in life; can be an urgent need to be out of the woods in a situation; feeling lost in the crowd; one's growth in life; depending on the context it can be a place of danger and darkness in your life where you could easily be spiritually lost or harmed; a feeling of confusion; feeling a lack of direction; uncultivated and undeveloped potential.

Forest Ranger: a helper.

Forest Fire: danger; disaster; judgement; God doing a major work in burning the junk out of your life.

Former Place: a season you are presently in or will be coming out of.

Fort / Fortress: a place of safety in battle; can also mean a strong enemy presence in your life.

Foundation: foundational Biblical teaching; your true beliefs you live your life by.

A to Z Christian Dream Symbols Dictionary

Fortune Teller: a person with satanic influence in your life; a demon wanting to plant a false word in your life.

Fountain: a life giving source; a source of refreshment; flowing wisdom.

Fox: a cunning spirit; a crafty person; being secretly counter-productive; a deceptive individual; little things in your life that spoil your spiritual walk.

Fox Cub: tiny problems.

Frame: a person's life being built or a ministry being built; can be your frame of mind which can be good or bad depending on the context.

Fred Flintstone Car: exhausting human effort instead of rest in God and being Holy Spirit empowered.

Freezer: storing spiritual food for a future time; feeling put on ice in ministry or life.

Friend: a person who is helpful and understanding; a brother or sister in Christ, or someone showing to have similar qualities; a faithful person; yourself.

Friendly Dog: you have a friend who will take care of or help you; someone is going to befriend you or you are to befriend someone.

Frog: an evil spirit; a noisy person; a boastful person; sorcery; a lying nature or spirit; someone speaking curses; someone plagued with unclean spirits.

Front Line: being at the point of attack in spiritual warfare; being at the front line for human or spiritual advancement.

Front porch: a time or place of vision; a place of fellowship; looking ahead; something in the future.

Fruit: good results or blessings; God's blessings; Christ's love for

His bride.

Fruit (Rotten): abandonment; curses; people with bad character.

Fuel: a source of energy; food for the Spirit; power and authority for ministry or to get through a circumstance; capable of reviving or being revived.

Fumble: dropping the ball; making a critical mistake.

Funeral: death or despair over the end of a situation or desire; can be death of sin, a habit or an addiction in your life.

Funeral Procession: mourning over the death of something in your life; mourning over lost opportunities or dreams.

Furnace: your heart; the source of heated and painful experiences; a fiery period of trial; a place of strong testing; God's judgment upon His enemies.

G

Gallows: place of judgment or punishment; a place of death to a problem or situation; death of a ministry or business; death of a relationship.

Games: living the game of life; thinking life is just a game.

Gangs/Gangsters: a gang of demons.

Gap: a breach or weak spot in your spiritual life; a loophole or an opening to walk through for good or to escape.

Garage: storage of dreams and hopes; a place of healing of life hurts; place of potential or protection.

Garbage: something to reject as worthless; something the Lord wants you to discard; abandoned things; corruption; reprobate; an unclean spirit; something that is thrown away or should be thrown away; opinions of life without Jesus; departure from all that is Godly; garbage on your face can mean rejection.

Garbage Truck: sin; worthless things or habits you need to get rid of.

Garden: a field of labor in life; a ministry or good soil to sow into; a place of increase or growth, fruitfulness and productivity; a place of rest; a place of intimacy; a place of love or romance.

Gardening: an area of ministry; a time of reward; a time of increase or harvest; the process of sowing and reaping.

Garment: a covering; a mantle; protection.

Garter Snake: a human or spiritual enemy that is relatively harmless and easily resisted.

Gasoline: God your source of energy and power; faith filled prayer; can be fuel for your ministry.

Gas Station: a place to energize or re-energize you or a situation; a potential dangerous situation; sinful motives; someone adding fuel to an explosive situation; fuel for the fire can be good or bad depending on the context.

Gas Station (Old): old power; outdated beliefs; outdated methods.

Gate: an opportunity requiring permission to enter; an opening for ministry; salvation; an entry point for angels or demons; a place of council.

Gate (Closed): shutting something or someone out of your life; closing the door on the past.

Gathering: wise counsel in a multitude of counselors; a church.

Gavel: a determined or final judgment for or against you.

Gazelle: swiftness; symbolic of a lover or a fiancé.

Gecko: feeling unnoticed; feeling small in spiritual stature or value.

Gems: high value in the spirit or natural realm.

General: a high-ranking military chief either good or evil depending on the context.

Get up and Go Somewhere, but Wake Up in Dream and Realize You Went Nowhere: you are afraid of someone or something; you are afraid you are going to miss something; you are afraid

A to Z Christian Dream Symbols Dictionary

you are not going to fulfill or complete something; there is anxiety in your heart about something or someone.

Ghosts: demonic spirits.

Giant: a powerful angel or demon; a challenging situation that needs to be overcome; a strongman; a champion for God; a stronghold either good or bad; a major challenge or obstacle; major trouble; an overwhelming person, situation or demon opponent.

Gifts: spiritual gifts; coming reward or opportunities; God's love.

Girdle: preparing for spiritual battle; might; potency; being strengthened for life's challenges; gathering the strength within you to face a person or situation.

Girl Scout: a helpful or courteous person.

Glass: a fragile person or situation; a transparent person or ministry; clarity of spiritual sight and vision.

Glasses/Contacts: a need for corrected spiritual vision.

Globe: Earth and its people.

Glue: symbolic of peace; togetherness in life or ministry; someone who brings people together in unity and strength.

Glutton: poverty; poverty spirit; glutton spirit.

Gloves: an opportunity or ministry that fits you; submitting to and allowing Holy Spirit to wear you as a glove; something or someone helping you to be productive and successful.

Gloves (Boxing): means you are ready to do battle and knock demonic spirits out of your or another's life .

Goal Keeper: someone resisting something which can be good or bad depending on what is being resisted.

Goat: feeling you are a scapegoat; foolish person; carnal; fleshly; not submitting to authority; walking into sin; a need for repentance; a miscarriage of judgment or justice; the lost or unsaved.

God: the heavenly Father is often symbolized by one's earthly father; a fathers love.

Going Bald: the loss of spiritual covering in one's life; a lack of wisdom.

Golden Bowl: the prayers of the saints.

Golden calf: idolatry in one's life.

Golden Cup: being used by God.

Golden Image: means there is an idol in your or another's life.

Golf: symbolic of your life; a hole in one represents success in your natural or spiritual life; if you are playing poorly it indicates disorder in your life.

Gong: doing works without love; a uncaring person or spirit.

Goodness: God's character; fruit of Holy Spirit.

Gorilla: a potentially strong or dangerous situation or problem.

Government: a call to pray for man's government; a call to pray for God's government to prevail.

Governor: a person who has power in a place or situation; a spiritual leader in the church; an evil principality; authority; Christ.

Grade: indicates how well you are doing in a certain area of your life.

Grain: God's provision and blessing; words; actions or things you are sowing in the field of life.

A to Z Christian Dream Symbols Dictionary

Grandchild: a blessing; a crown; a spirit either good or bad passed on from previous generation; a generational inheritance either good or bad; natural and spiritual heirs; spiritual offspring of your ministry.

Grandmother: generational authority over a person; a spiritual inheritance; past wisdom or gifting.

Grapes: something valuable; a prized position; God's Word in seed form; fruit of God's promises to you; sour grapes indicate sin in your life; a sour disposition, a soured life.

Grass: green pastures of God; life; something meant to be maintained in your spiritual life.

Grass Dried: death of the flesh through repentance; fruit of dead or wrong works.

Grass Mowed: disciplined obedience.

Grasshopper/Locust: a devastating situation; an instrument of God's judgment; low self-esteem; old age.

Grass Snake: see snakes.

Grave/Graveyard: burying or laying to rest an issue or desire; death to old desires, death to old tradition; cultural reserve; natural death; demonic influence from the past.

Gravel: indicates stolen goods; gravel in your mouth means being conquered.

Gray Hair: wisdom; a crown of glory.

Grenade: a sudden explosive person or situation.

Grim Reaper: a call to pray against a literal and untimely death; can also mean death of a ministry, business or desire.

Grinding Wheel: someone or something is wearing your down, physically, emotionally or spiritually.

Grocery: a person, place or ministry that provides spiritual nourishment.

Groom: Jesus the Bridegroom; marriage; headship.

Ground: readiness of someone to receive the gospel; you are on the ground floor of a breakthrough or advancement; if the ground is dry it means spiritual barrenness.

Growling: dissatisfied and wicked people.

Guard/S: God's servants or angels; an ability to keep on the right path; a spirit of protection; you are to be vigilant and guarded; if the guard is dressed in black it means demonic oppression and torment.

Guest: spiritual messenger either an angel or a demon.

Guide: God; Holy Spirit; a righteous person; can also mean demonic spirit guides depending on the context.

Guitar: worship; praise; joyfulness.

Gum: chewing gum indicates immaturity.

Guns: spiritual authority either good or bad; an instrument of demonic affliction; spoken words that wound; the power of your words in prayer; dominion through speaking the Word of God; if holding the gun it means your spiritual power and authority; can be weapons people use against one another such as curses, hurtful words, lies, slander or insults.

Gun (Empty): means no spiritual power.

Gun (Battery Powered): means weak or limited power or power of short duration.

Gun (Cap Gun): all noise but no spiritual power; a form of godliness but no power.

A to Z Christian Dream Symbols Dictionary

Gun (Water): shooting or releasing Holy Spirit at someone.

Gun:(Pistol): gossiping; slander; words used as weapons.

Gun (Cannon): a major far reaching verbal assault; a major demonic attack.

Gun (Machine): a multitude of hateful and harmful words coming against you; your spiritual weaponry against the enemy.

Gunslinger: someone who uses the word of God skillfully in a spiritual fight; negatively it can mean someone skillful in using words for harm and destruction.

Gymnasium: strengthening your spirit through prayer and the Word of God; strong spiritual discipline; you are allowing God to deal with you and it is something you are going to do over and over again.

Gymnastics: hard work through much practice that produces great spiritual results.

Gypsy/Vagrant: never settles down or commits.

H

Hail: judgment against God's enemies; sudden war declared by God with a promise of victory if we pray.

Hail Mary: long odds for a positive outcome in a situation; a last ditch effort in a situation.

Hair: a spiritual covering; something numerous either good or bad in your life; man's glory; wisdom.

Baldness: grief and shame; a lack of wisdom.

Haircut: getting something in correct condition; cutting off a habit or tradition.

Long Hair (Maintained): covenant and strength.

Long Hair (Man): rebellious behavior; a covenant relationship.

Long Hair (Woman): glory on the woman; church submission.

Long Unkempt Hair: out of control.

Losing Hair: loss of wisdom; loss of glory.

Shaving: getting rid of what hinders or what is sinful in your life.

Short Hair: losing wisdom if a woman; not submitting.

To Shape: to acquire wisdom.

Half Man-Half Animal: a demon trying to control or influence you.

A to Z Christian Dream Symbols Dictionary

Hall: your path in life; life choices; a long and monotonous journey.

Hallway of Doors: many choices and opportunities.

Hall of Fame: heroes of faith; negatively it can mean pride.

Halo: holiness.

Hammer: the Living Word; preaching the Word hard and fast; capable of breaking up a situation that is bad; a militant person, a group or nation.

Hamster: someone is going in circles and getting nowhere.

Hand: a means of service or expressing strength; direction for life.
Clapping: joy and worship.

Fist: pride in one's strength.

Hands Covering Face: guilt or shame.

Holding Hands: agreement.

Left Hand: something spiritual; riches; wisdom; honor; if the person is evil it means wicked scheming and bribery.

Raised Hand: surrender or worshiping.

Right Hand: oath of allegiance; means of power and honor; strength and victory; long life.

Shaking Hands: coming to an agreement.

Stretched out Hands: surrender.

Trembling Hands: being fearful; a spirit of fear; anxiety; awe at God's presence.

Hands Under Thighs: oaths.

Washing Hands: declaring innocence; to dissociate oneself from a person, habit or sin.

Handcuffs: someone or something restricting your behavior or progress; the power to bind or stop certain actions or behavior.

Hanging on: a long wait for help or change; feeling you are barely hanging on in life.

Happiness: possessing wisdom; the joy of the Lord.

Harbor: shelter; a place of safety.

Harlot or Prostitute: seduction; fornication; rebellion; loudness; a snare; a tempting situation or person; something that appeals to your flesh; worldly desires; a former bad habit that wants to be resurrected; enticement.

Harp: if used for God it means praise and worship in Heaven and on Earth; you are an instrument for praise and worship; the joy of the Lord.

Harvest: gathering; seasons of Grace; opportunities to share the gospel; fruitfulness; spiritual reward of labor and action.

Hat: symbol of authority for women; a covering; protection; a crown.

Hatchet: smashing; destroying; cutting off sinful habits; cutting off your past.

Hawks: something unclean trying to land on you, especially if the hawk is grey or black.

Hazard Sign: a warning to stop something or not do something; a hazardous situation; danger ahead.

Head: lordship; authority; Jesus or God; a husband; a master or boss; a pastor; your mind; your thoughts; if something is on your head it indicates either God's blessings or a curse depending on the context; a faceless head can signify all of humanity.

A to Z Christian Dream Symbols Dictionary

Anointed Head: set apart for God's service.

Hand Covering the Head: signifying sorrow.

Head Usher: represents tradition.

Health: the Word of God.

Hearse: bringing death of a relationship, person or situation.

Heart: the condition of our life or intents; an upside down heart indicates distress and anxiety over troubles or situations in life

Heckler: a scoffer; an ungodly person.

Hedge: God's protection and security; safety; if the hedge is made of thorns it indicates a lazy person.

Hedgehog: solitude; separation.

Heel: a crushing power.

Helicopter: Holy Spirit powered for spiritual warfare; a one man ministry; a fast paced lifestyle; someone who parties, drinks and uses drugs.

Hell: eternal punishment; part of your soul being held in captivity by the demonic.

Helmet: an awareness and inner assurance of salvation; God's promises; protection of authority.

Hemorrhage: losing one's faith, livelihood or strength; a need to have faith in Christ.

Herbs: love; goodness; nutrition; if bitter herbs it can mean grief.

Herd: may indicate the condition of your property or wealth.

Hiding: indicates a prudent person; could mean hiding from problems; trying to hide sin or wrong habits; trying to hide from God.

High rise building: see office building.

High school: moving into a higher level of your walk with God; you are capable of moving others into a higher walk with God.

Highway: the Holy way; the path of life; the truth of God; Christ; a predetermined path of life or a path of life that enjoys high volume usage, which may lead to good or evil destinations.

Dead End: a course of action that will lead to nothing gained.

Gravel Road: God's word; stony ground or heart.

Muddy Road: on a difficult path in life; an un-clear life path; an uncertain path.

Road with Construction: in a preparation time; change is coming.

Hiking: challenges in life; willing to minister in difficult areas.

Hills: a place of exaltation; an easily overcome obstacle; can indicate a place in life where you can build, work and cultivate good things in your life; a brightly lit hill indicates God's dwelling place; you are being uplifted high above the natural into the spiritual realm; the throne of God; Mount Zion.

Hindu gods: indicates someone filled with Eastern religious beliefs.

Hippopotamus: a dangerous person who has a big mouth in verbal attacks.

Hips: reproduction or relating to reproduction; you are being a support to someone.

Hissing: a harassing spirit; a condemning spirit.

A to Z Christian Dream Symbols Dictionary

Hitting: hitting others in a dream means you have anger directed towards others; if you are hitting yourself it means you are angry at yourself or have regrets.

Holding hands: being in agreement with someone; keeping in touch with someone; a symbol of God's faithfulness, protection and love.

Hole: a pit in life to avoid; a death trap; a prostitute; a hiding place, if the hole is in a garment it means there are things in your life that need repair.

Home Run: sliding home safe from the enemy; running home to God; winning the game of life.

Homeless Person: an evil spirit searching for a home or to steal from you; a wandering spirit.

Homosexual: in a dream it means a perverse spirit or person.

Honey: sweetness in life or with God; the law, teaching, testimony and judgments of God.

Honeycomb: pleasant speech; kind words; healing.

Horn: symbolic of power; source of anointed power; the power of kings and leaders; a call to war in prayer; negatively it means boasting and pride.

Honking horn: an impatient person; a warning of danger.

Hornets: being spiritually confused; being blindsided or stung by someone; attacking demonic spirits of terror and confusion.

Horse: great strength and power and the context will tell if bad or good power; you are powerful in spiritual warfare; you have a spirit of tenacity; not double minded; a powerful ministry capable of competing against the enemy; strength in humility and meekness; God's judgment; strength for the battle; the means of fast travel in in the spirit and to battle.

Horse (Flame Colored Bay) power; fire.

Horse (Black): lack.

Horse (Pale): spirit of death.

Horse (Red): danger; passion; the blood of Jesus.

Horse (White): purity; righteousness; Christ's return.

Horse (Kicks/Kicking): threats; opposition.

Horse (Blue): spiritual.

Horse (Brown): repentant; born again.

Horse (Grey): vague or hazy; neither hot nor cold; double minded.

Horse (Orange): danger; evil.

Horse (Pink): flesh; desires and decisions based on the mind or flesh.

Horse (Purple): related to royalty or to be treated as royalty; noble character; riches.

Horse (Yellow): gift from God; cowardness or fear.

Hospital: healing anointing; caring; loving; edifying others; a place of healing; a healing ministry or church.

Hotel: a place of gathering; a temporary place of meeting; a church; a temporary situation, a temporary provision; a temporary location.

Hourglass: fleeting time and deadlines; running out of time; a need to better manage your time.

House: one's spiritual and emotional house; one's personality; actual or church family; a house of prayer; a symbol of one's choices; a person tearing down a house is symbolic of a fool.

A to Z Christian Dream Symbols Dictionary

House (Crumbling): indicates a wicked person.

House Filled with Good Things: indicates a wise person.

House made of Cards or Flimsy Materials: indicates folly.

House Build on Sand: indicates coming disaster.

House Burned With Only a Picture Left: the picture will determine what it means; can be a family or church family issue and the enemy may try or has tried to ravage the home.

Hovering: see floating

Howling (Wolves): an evil person or a demon trying to bring fear.

Hummingbird: busy; industrious; flighty.

Hunger: a spiritual desire; spiritually malnourished.

Hunter: having the upper hand in a situation.

Hurricane: distress; sudden disaster and trouble in a person's life.

Husband: an actual husband; Jesus Christ; if an ex-husband it can mean someone or something that had control over you in the past.

Hut: placing your faith and trust in something flimsy or unsafe.

Hyena: indicates a person or a demon who pursues and harasses people; someone is ridiculing, mocking or laughing at you, or you are doing the same to another.

Hyssop: a need for cleansing; faith in Christ.

I

Ice: in danger of losing one's footing or way; someone who is cool, calm and collected in a stressful situation.

Ice Cream: enjoying the milk of God's Word; joy; happiness; fun.

Ice Water: good news; receiving refreshment when spiritually parched; helping to cool down a tense situation or person.

Iceberg: a hidden or unforeseen emerging danger.

ICU: a need to have spiritual or emotional intensive care; needing major help.

Icy Path or Road: if you are slipping on an icy path it indicates the path of the arrogant and wicked; you are proceeding too fast in a situation.

Idols: distractions to keep from serving God.

Immunization: a need for strength to resist spiritual infirmities; building character and strength to resist temptation.

Implant: something in your life did not originate with you.

Impound: stopping someone's progress in life; capturing someone's heart usually in a negative sense.

Incense: the sweet aroma of prayer; worship; praise; being acceptable to God; a call to prayer.

Incest: influence by a family member's perversions; influence

A to Z Christian Dream Symbols Dictionary

from a spirit of perversion.

Incisor Teeth: see teeth.

Income: finances related to work or ministry.

Index finger: prophetic or a prophetic calling.

Indians: may indicate pride; a call to prayer for sins against Native Americans.

Infant: early stage of an idea; a new thing; a young believer's need for the foundations of faith.

Inheritance: indicates a good person; a spiritual blessings from one generation to another; negatively it can mean inheriting a generational curse or iniquity.

Injury: spiritual or emotional wounding; an incurable injury indicates a deep rooted sin in one's life.

Insurance: a need to be assured of God and His Word; a need to insulate or protect yourself from someone or something.

Interior Designer: getting your house in order spiritually or relationally.

Investigator: being wise and honorable; diligently searching out the things of God.

Invitation: a request from God to you for intimacy.

In School and Can't Unlock Your Locker: someone or something is trying to stop you from getting the necessary tools to complete what God has called you to do.

Iron: an inflexible person; a person or object with strength and powerful; strict rules; powerful strongholds; accountability in Christian growth.

Ironing: process of correction by instructions; teaching; talk

John Mark Volkots

matters over; working out wrinkles in relationships and in your life; turning from sin.

Iron bars: someone or something trying to bar you from your destiny or calling; a feeling of imprisonment; arguments.

Iron Rod: judgment.

Island: something related to the island such as its name or what it is known for; seclusion or seasonal isolation; a hiding place in God.

Israel: a call to pray for Israel; a call to pray for the Jews to receive their Messiah; the redeemed; the body of Christ.

Ivory: luxury and lavishness.

J

Jackal: an evil scoffer.

Jacket: being protected or being a protection for others; spiritual covering.

Jail: feeling imprisoned in a situation; feeling a loss of freedoms; being bound or imprisoned mentally or spiritually.

Jail keeper: a demonic or human oppressor.

Janitor: a servant who cleans up others' emotional messes; humble circumstances; a servant; an official position of trust.

Javelin: war.

Jawbone: supernatural spiritual and emotional strength; someone using their jaws to slander, hurt or trap you.

Jaws (Trap): entrapment.

Jaws (Mouth): someone jawing or speaking against you or another.

Jeans: completing your calling.

Jellybeans: immaturity in a person; a desire for pleasures in life.

Jerusalem: a place of peace; a city chosen by God; the city of God a place of praise.

Jester: one who brings joy to others; a jokester; someone who can't be taken seriously; a slanderer.

Jesus: an invitation to salvation, healing, deliverance or restoration.

Jet: see airplanes.

Jewels: true riches of heaven; valuable possessions; God's people; a person God has gifted; a valued object or person; rewards and favor, especially if the jewels are set in a crown.

Jogging: a relaxing pace in life; a ministry that flows effortlessly.

Journey/Trip: you path in life toward your destiny in God.

Joy or Someone Named Joy: happiness and joy in the Spirit; God's favor and fruit of the Spirit.

Judge: God The Father; an authority figure; one anointed to make good decisions; Jesus; someone who can decide your fate; can also indicate trouble with earthly authorities.

Judges Bench: the judgment seat of Christ; God's courtroom in heaven to bring justice for you and against your enemies.

Juggling: over activity; feeling overwhelmed; having to do too many things at once.

Jugular Vein (Being Cut): a spiritual, emotional or physical threat to you; someone or something draining your emotional or spiritual energy.

Jungle Gym: playing around in life; not being serious about spiritual matters.

Junk: reading or watching worthless material; involved in worthless activity; allowing sin and garbage in your life.

Junk food: listening to advice that has little or no value; improper spiritual diet; a call to read God's Word and pray more.

Junkyard: a feeling you have been discarded or placed on a shelf by God or others; a place to discard sins, lusts, worthless emotions, beliefs or lifestyles.

Jury: someone passing judgment on you or you passing judgment on others.

Junior Varsity: not yet proven to handle greater spiritual warfare.

K

Kamikaze: recklessness; someone or something doomed for failure because of their actions or lifestyle.

Kangaroo: something not based on truth; rushing to a conclusion; prejudiced.

Karate: skilled in spiritual warfare.

Keg: drunkenness and sin.

Kernel: seemingly small or insignificant beginnings but with great potential.

Keyhole: needing the right key for a way in or out of a situation.

Keys: spiritual authority over the demonic world; a way to unlock doors of opportunity or progress; a critical or crucial element needed to do something in your life.

Kicking: self-regret; being on the defensive in a struggle; kicking against God's will for your life; kicking others is anger directed to another person.

Kidnapped/Kidnapper: being taken somewhere emotionally or in the spirit realm against your will; someone or something keeping you in a situation against your will; an evil spirit trying to keep you bound in emotional or spiritual captivity.

Killer: an evil spirit that is out to destroy your destiny, dreams and success.

Killing: killing someone can be suppressed anger; fear or jeal-

A to Z Christian Dream Symbols Dictionary

ousy towards another person.

Kiln: being hardened in your heart or conscious as a result of sin; a place of waiting and gaining strength under heat.

Kindness: God's favor and fruit of the Spirit.

King: a person in supreme authority; it can represent Jesus and God.

King Cobra: see snakes.

Kiss/Kissing: intimacy; coming into agreement; seduction; enticement; deception or betrayal; betrayed by a friend or brother or sister in Christ.

Kitchen: your home life; serving others; working hard to spiritually nourish others; a hunger for God or His Word; worrying too much;

Kite (Flying on a String): earthly prayer tethered to unseen answers in heaven.

KKK: prejudice and racism.

Kneeling: surrender; submission; a call to prayer.

Knees: your prayer life; a call to prayer.

Knife/Sword: your spiritual weapons; the Word of God; using your voice and cutting words as a weapon to speak against someone; an ability to cut spiritual meat into bite-size pieces for teaching.

Knight: a person you think highly of or have a romantic interest in; a rescuer or deliverer; Jesus.

Knocking: you are trying to get an entrance into an area or situation; something or someone trying to gain entrance in your life; an invitation of Jesus; negatively it can be a demon trying to gain entrance into your life.

John Mark Volkots

Knockout: winning a battle.

L

Labor: birthing a business, ministry or something in life through intense physical or spiritual emotional effort, strain or pain

Labyrinth/Maze: feeling lost, confused and trapped in life or a situation

Ladder: a changing spiritual condition or position either good or bad depending if you are going up or down; escaping from emotional or spiritual captivity; occupational or spiritual promotion; greater closeness to God if ascending.

Lady Bugs: little irritations; little harassing spirits; God is going to eliminate what is harassing you.

Lake: your environment or surroundings; if the water is clear you are in a good spiritual place in life; if dirty or murky you are in a bad environment or place in your spiritual life.

Lamb/Sheep: Christ; young children; baby believers; believers; gentleness; blamelessness.

Lame: shortcomings; feeling you are not able or equipped to do what is expected or you; a flaw in your walk with God; limitations placed on you by others or yourself.

Lamp/Lantern: refers to our eyes and our Christian walk; being a source of light to others; our spirit man; the Holy Spirit; revelation; the Word of God.

Land: you; your spiritual inheritance; your sphere of influence; a promise given by God.

Bare Earth or Dust: a curse; barrenness.

Neglected/Unwanted Land: a neglected promise or inheritance.

Newly Cleared Land: new revelation; cleaned of garbage in your life.

Ripe Fruit or Produce on the Land: fruitful work of the ministry.

Large House: a large family or large church family; where we work or go to church if brick.

Laser: spiritual sight that pierces the darkness; pinpoint spiritual insight; able to zero in on a problem in a situation.

Las Vegas: a seat of sin; spiritual Sodom and Gomorrah.

Laugh/Laughing: God's superiority over His enemies; rejoicing; the joy of the Lord; outburst of excitement or joy over something good that happened or will happen; if others are laughing at you it indicates arrogance or sarcasm.

Laundry: airing your sin or the secrets of your heart.

Lawn Mower: keeping your life clean of sin.

Lava: the enemy creeping in; slow destruction and judgment; slow destruction because of a wrong lifestyle or belief.

Lawyer: a mediator; Jesus Christ; can indicate legalism; the accuser of the brethren.

La-Z-Boy Recliner: a slothful person; laziness; at rest and peace.

Lead (Metal): a heavy burden or yoke in life; a weighty situation.

Leaf: a time of change in life; a fragile situation; a changing situation or opportunity.

A to Z Christian Dream Symbols Dictionary

Leak: a pesky problem in your life; a leaking roof indicates idleness.

Leaking: a potential loss; situations or problems that are draining you physically or spiritually; someone leaking confidential things about your life.

Leash: someone or something placing restrictions or limitations on you.

Leaven: unrighteousness; sin spreading others; a false belief system; hypocrisy; Pharisee spirit or influence.

Leaves: healing of the nations;

Leaves (Healthy Leaves): being planted in the river of life.

Leaves (Dry): dry in the Spirit; under pressures of life.

Leech: a person who is draining to others physically, emotionally or spiritually.

Left: that which is of the Spirit; God manifested through the flesh of man; gifts and talents you were born with.

Left turn: the opposite of a right turn is a wrong turn or decision in life; the path of foolishness.

Legs: being a support to others; spiritual strength to walk through life; female legs can mean seduction or the power to entice.

Lemon: a bitter situation that is not to your liking; bitter doctrine; something gone or going sour.

Lens/Eye Glasses: your perspective; your opinion; how you see others.

Leopard: solitude or seclusion; may represent a sudden evil ambush.

Leprosy: feeling rejection or being an outcast.

Letter: pay attention to the message if it is addressed to you; if addressed to others it may be things you want to say but never had the chance to say them.

Leviathan: a powerful demonic spirit; pride; rebellion; a major problem or situation can only be eliminated by the power of God.

Library: you are searching for information or knowledge; a love of knowledge; a place of knowledge; schooling; wisdom; a great desire for the knowledge of God's will.

Lice: accusation; shame; a concerted attempt to smear you; lice on your head means an excessive compulsion to lie.

Licking Dust: enemies of God and they will eventually lick the dust.

Lie Detector Test: the presence of deceit; the need for truthfulness; being caught in a lie.

Life Insurance: a desire for salvation; assurance of salvation.

Life Guard: protecting or watching out for others.

Life Jacket: rescue during desperate times.

Light: being in the dark and then having a light turned on is God showing you that righteous living will illuminate your life or situation; God is light; no longer hidden; enlightenment to God's Word..

Absence of Light: a lack of understanding; an absence of God in your life; satan and the demonic realm.

Dim Light: showing a need for deeper intimacy and knowledge of God and His Word.

A to Z Christian Dream Symbols Dictionary

Small Lamp or Flashlight: only walking in partial founding of the Word.

Lightbulb: a bright or creative idea; revelation; wisdom.

Lighthouse: direction in times of trouble; God preventing shipwreck or disaster in your life or ministry; hope when searching.

Lightning: God's voice; God interrupting an activity to get our attention; something happening or will happen suddenly; revelation; supernatural power.

Lightning Eyes: a demonic or angelic spirit being.

Lilies: young girls; blossoming in life.

Limbs not working right: if your legs or arms won't straighten out it can mean a gifting or anointing is not fully operating yet and you are just limping along.

Limousine: a call of God; being carried to your next assignment by God; pride.

Limp-Handed: weak; no influence; powerlessness.

Limping: having wrestled with God and been humbled; not operating in full Holy Spirit power.

Lion: Jesus; the conquering nature of Jesus; a powerful spirit either good or bad; a prowling enemy or demon if the lion is intimidating and aggressive.

Lion's Den: a very public and dangerous place of testing.

Lips: the Word of God; an offering; a means of testifying; speaking falsehood or accusation; seduction through smooth words; if dripping with honey it can mean seductive words and enticement; unclean speech.

Lipstick: rich lips and speech; beautifying yourself in the spirit.

105

Litmus Paper: testing to establishing true character.

Liver: discernment as a filter for yourself or others.

Livestock: plenty of provision; may mean dealing with real stocks in the stock market.

Lizard: a familiar spirit; if a creature with a human face it means a person with a nasty disposition is in your life.

Living Room: part of your personality that is open for others to see.

Load: can be sin or anxieties in your life; a heavy load can also mean you carry other people's problems.

Lock: a situation or something that is sealed or cannot be opened without God's permission; a situation requiring a key of wisdom to gain entry or exit.

Lockers: unable to lock or unlock your locker in school means something or someone is trying to stop you from learning a life lesson.

Locker Room: coaching or preparing for a major event in your life.

Locusts: many enemies attacking you; demonic spirits trying to devour something in your life; a swarming evil demonic army.

Log: hypocrisy; problems you cannot see.

Lone Wolf: feeling as an outsider or rejected; a person who wants to do everything alone; an independent spirit.

Long Jump: reaching for a distant goal.

Looting: being overrun by physical or spiritual enemies.

Lost (Direction): indicates inner confusion or indecision.

A to Z Christian Dream Symbols Dictionary

Lottery: sudden financial gain; a physical, emotional or spiritual blessing; taking risky chances in life.

Love: God's character; the fruit of Holy Spirit; pure affection.

Luggage: baggage from your past; preparing to move on in life or destiny; a traveling ministry.

Lukewarm Water: spiritual compromise, lethargy or passivity,

Lungs: life and breath; praise.

Lurking: physical or spiritual enemies lurking in your life for harm.

Lust: lustful dreams are demonic; may reveal lust in your heart.

Lying: a lying spirit demonic spirit; God may be telling you that someone is not being truthful to you or you are not being truthful to someone.

Lynch Mob: a group of people who hate you; a group of people who wrongly want to take matters into their own hands.

M

Machines: power and mechanism of the spirit realm; you may be living in a cold emotional environment; you may be trying to suppress your emotions.

Maggot: a wicked person; can mean rotten thinking or beliefs; defeat; death.

Magic/Magician: witchcraft; divination; deceiving spirits; fraud; deception; a person being used by demonic forces to manipulate a situation.

Magnifying Glass: close examination of something or someone.

Maid: servanthood; someone who cleans up other's messes in prayer.

Mailbox: God or a person wanting to send you a message; a prophetic ministry; a place where prophetic messages are delivered.

Mailman: a messenger; a prophet.

Makeup: self-improvement; making yourself beautiful in the spirit; trying to cover your flaws; trying to avoid being vulnerable.
Mall: a large church or many faceted ministry; egotism; selfishness; can also be choices in life.

Mamba: an evil spirit.

Man (Unknown or No Face): Jesus; angels; an evil messenger, a demon.

Mane: maturity.

Manger: humble beginnings; the birth of Christ.

Manna: the Glory of God; the Bread of Life; supernatural provision from God or from an unknown source.

Mansion: your heavenly place in God.

Mantle: authority; an office; a position; ranking; the color of the mantle will give insight; if someone is wearing it, can mean an angel bringing you a message.

Manual Labor: making money or a profit.

Manure: hard labor; dirty work; being admonished by God; filth; something unpleasant in your life that can promotes emotional or spiritual growth.

Map: the Word of God; instruction and direction for life; a literal location; if the roads are crooked it can mean a sinful lifestyle; getting to your spiritual destination requires following God's roadmap.

Marathon: a coming army in unison or unity.

Marble: beauty; the majesty of God.

Marching: an army either good or bad depending on the context.

Marionette: a person is being controlled by a person, a demonic or an organization.

Mark: something that distinguishes; a symbol; being set apart; the mark of God or the devil.

Market: symbolic of the world; business; profit.

Marriage: going deeper into the things of God; a covenant; an actual marriage; Jesus and the church; dreaming of marriage can mean working together or a desire to be married.

Marsh: the grave; death or destruction of something in your life.

Mascara: anything to do with eyes suggests improving vision or creative perspective; negatively can mean seduction or allurement.

Mask: a disguise; deception; deceit; trying to hide who you are.

Matador: taking high risk chances with your life.

Match (Fire): someone who starts arguments.

Mattress: a need to rest more physically; a need to find rest in God.

Maze: feeling lost; feeling trapped in life.

Measuring Stick: examining someone or something to see if they measure up.

Meat: strong doctrine; spiritual nourishment for the mature; important spiritual truths; meat of the matter.

Meat Hook: being dragged along against your will.

Mecca: Islamic or Middle East influence.

Medal: reward; honor or recognition.

Medical Exam: a need for spiritual or emotional introspection; can be a warning from God to show you a physical injury or illness about yourself or another; a warning from God that you need to examine your spiritual condition.

Medicine: a joyful heart; a need for prayer; a need for physical, emotional or spiritual healing; God's remedy for a situation or problem.

A to Z Christian Dream Symbols Dictionary

Melting: resignation or a loss of resolve over a situation; a loss of one's firm beliefs.

Menorah: Israel; God's chosen people; a call to pray for Israel.

Menstruation: stress and anxiety of not feeling presentable; purification; may be message of timing of some event in your life.

Mental Hospital: having issues with depression; fear of or feeling overwhelmed in life; internal conflict with overwhelming emotional confusion.

Mental Patient: an out of control lifestyle; a demonic attack on your life; feeling out of control in life.

Menu: one's options or choices in life.

Mercenary: a spiritual enemy who specializes in attacking believers.

Merchant: the offering Jesus to a dying world; God's warning that others or you are using the church or the gospel for gain; God may be opening a door for you in the business world to prosper you; God calling you to take Jesus to the market place.

Mercy Seat: God's love and mercy; God Himself; the Kingship of the Lord; the throne of God.

Meteor: coming physical or emotional adversity or attack that will impact your life, indicating a need for prayer.

Mice/Rats: demons that eat away at your life little by little; rats mean larger and more authoritative demonic attacks that feed off of garbage that you allowed in your life; demonic spirits also get in because something was left unattended as they come in through holes and cracks in your spiritual walls through unclean choices.

Microphone/Megaphone: the Word of God amplified in your life

111

or through you to others; preaching; a prophetic ministry; an ability to influence many people.

Microscope: a need to look more carefully at your lifestyle; a need to look closely at the little things in your life that have negative effects; you are magnifying or blowing out of proportion a situation or circumstance; ungodly intense examination yourself or others.

Microwave Oven: a lack of patience; looking for an easy option; a quick acting process or situation coming in your life.

Middle/Junior High: medium level equipping by God.

Midnight: a time to pray for others while they sleep; time to praise and thank God.

Mildew/Mold: a curse or curses to be broken off your life.

Milk: God's Word; good spiritual nourishment; elementary teaching.

Millstone: being weighed down with sin, grief or life burdens; feeling life is weighing you down.

Military Uniform: the Lord's army; a believer ready for spiritual battle; ready or a call to be ready for spiritual battles.

Minefield: concealed dangers; human or spiritual traps and obstacles.

Mining: digging for God's wisdom and truths; seeing the good in yourself or others; desiring earthly treasures.

Mint: exact giving; being in good spiritual condition.

Mire: sinking in trials; coming under an overwhelming attack by your enemies; feeling trapped by your enemy; feeling stuck in life or in your spiritual condition.

A to Z Christian Dream Symbols Dictionary

Mirrors: you are reflecting on a situation or circumstance; God is letting you know what is going on in your life; God or His Word revealing a need for change; feeling self-conscious; self-evaluation; God is letting you know your true image as He sees you; vanity or pride.

Miscarriage/Abortion: a discarded idea; an actual event of having aborted a baby; having your plans aborted; losing something at the beginning stages either good or bad; a desire, goal, project or destiny is being terminated.

Mischief: foolish behavior.

Missiles: a great bombardment from the demonic realm; your spiritual warfare prayers have great impact.

Missionary: literal or symbolic of ministry travels; a call to missions or to support missions.

Mist: the Spirit of God; something temporal, vanishing or fleeting.

Mobile Home: a temporary situation; changing homes; occupations or ministry direction.

Moccasin: see snakes.

Mold: something rotten in your life or attempting to come into your life; an unsalvageable situation or relationship.

Mole (Animal): hiding from trouble; hiding from responsibilities.

Mole (Skin Blemish): being self-conscious; if seeing moles on other people it means you are being judgmental and seeing their flaws.

Moldy Bread: a call to find fresh teaching; what you are eating spiritually is not healthy.

113

Monastery: seclusion; trying to hide yourself from the world; trying to avoid relationships.

Money: God's favor; spiritual and natural wealth; spiritual authority; man's power and strength; greed; favor or loss of favor; financial blessing and prosperity.

Monk/Nun: a life of chastity; hiding from others or God; a call to pray without ceasing.

Monkey/S: playfulness; childlike; one who harasses; overbearing; an oppressive spirit taking one captive—"monkey on his back".

Monster: a problem or spiritual enemy capable of swallowing or destroying your life, business or ministry; a demonic oppressor using intimidation to defeat; an actual person.

Moon: a symbol for a pagan deity; indicating ruler-ship; to reign in the night seasons; the light of God at a dark season of life.

Moon (Blood Colored): the church being persecuted; a time of significance; a sign either good or bad depending on the context.

Moon (Full): the end of a journey or a season of life; the end of life; also means a time for feasting, joy and praise; also indicates something that is established.

Mop: needing to clean one's life or path and walk with God; cleaning up other people's messes.

Morning: loving kindness; the beginning of something new; the light of God after a dark season of life; sins being revealed; rejoicing.

Mosque: symbol of Islam; Middle Eastern influence.

Motel: transient employment or position; a temporary time of learning; a temporary situation or condition.

Mortgage: a large debt.

A to Z Christian Dream Symbols Dictionary

Moth: transient wealth; something eating away at what you hold valuable; the demonic realm sneaking into areas of your life to destroy things that protect and insulate you; the demonic realm out to devour your possessions, physically and spiritually.

Mother: the church; Jerusalem; one's actual mother; a spiritual mother; a caregiver or teacher.

Mother-in-Law: a church that is not your actual church; a false teacher; one's actual mother-in-law.

Motor (Engine or Battery): the source of power and anointing.

Motorcycle: a small and efficient fast-moving ministry; a Spirit powered personal ministry; a loner; a show-off; pride or exhibitionism; a fast-paced or free-living lifestyle or individual.

Mountain: prosperity and favor of God on your life; great power and strength either for good or evil; a place of revelation or meeting with God and His glory; obstacles or troubles to overcome in the spirit and through prayer; can indicate a nation's or someone's life journey.

Mountain (Treacherous): obstacles or resistance to spiritual growth.

Mountain Top: high things in the spirit.

Mountain (Moving a Mountain): great faith in God.

Mourning/Mourners: spirits of grief and death; death to dreams or desires; an actual death.

Mouth: speaking evil or good words; something from which come the issues of life; can be words coming against you.

Mouth (Crooked): perverse speech.

Mouth (Silver): a righteous person.

Movie: desire to be entertained; show something literal; God revealing your life for you; pay attention to titles and actor's names, the plot and characters.

Movie Theater: being assembled with people of similar interests or activities; a desire to be entertained or to be entertaining.

Moving: a change in spiritual and emotional condition; a changing situation; imminent change; an actual move.

Moving (Van or Truck): transitioning in ministry; transitioning in life; a coming literal change of location.

Mud/Dirt: can mean being stained by sin; stuck in sin; or stuck in life.

Muddy Water: impure doctrine; stagnant living; a foul spiritual environment; someone or something muddying the water to make things less clear or pure.

Mule: an unbridled person; a stubborn person; can be a stubborn situation that that is difficult to move through.

Murder: jealousy; injustice; unrighteousness.

Murdered or Flogged: by unbelievers means persecution or coming persecution; being shot by someone in the church means words spoken against you by believers; if you died it means you died to yourself and flesh.

Murderer: a person or a demonic spirit seeking to destroy your life, your ministry, destiny or dreams.

Muscles: spiritual strength.

Mushroom Cloud: major spiritual warfare.

Music: praise and worship; flowing in spiritual gifts; teaching; admonishing; a message to be given or received.

A to Z Christian Dream Symbols Dictionary

Music Notes: the flow of life; if the notes are in harmony it indicates virtuous living or living in harmony with others; if the notes scream it indicates wickedness or disharmony in your life.

Musical Instruments: unity with diversity.

Musicians: unity in praising God; prophecy.

Muslim: possible Islamic influence.

Mustard or Mustard Seed: small beginnings; small faith; the value or power of even small faith; sowing in faith; the Word of God; God's promise.

Mute: the presence of a deaf and dumb spirit; feeling unable to defend or speak for yourself.

Muzzle: being forbidden to speak; guarding one's mouth from sin.

Myrrh: sacrificial death of Christ for us.

Myrtle Tree: God's provision in desperate times.

N

Nagging: a harassing spirit, a spirit of torment; an actual person nagging another.

Nails: making something more permanent; how Jesus permanently dealt with our sins.

Nail polish: beautifying yourself; preparing for battle or a big job ahead; vanity.

Naked: nothing hidden; without guile; being naked means you are being vulnerable and have placed yourself in a position where everyone can see what is going on in your life; God is going to make you transparent before people or you are already transparent before people; purity; shame; feeling uncovered; if embarrassment it shows a fear of being vulnerable, exposed or shamed.

Names: pray for those seen; to designate rank or status of someone; research name meaning for a message to yourself; if you see a name crumbling or rotting it indicates wickedness and evil.

Nation: can represent characteristics of the nation; a calling related to the nation, the actual nation.

America: proud; independent; prosperity.

France: romance.

Germany: hardworking; stubborn; precise.

Jews: business minded; God's people.

A to Z Christian Dream Symbols Dictionary

Native American: animism and worship of nature.

Nausea: in a bad environment; a person or place that will make you sick; a place of bad or evil activities.

Nazi: an oppressive person or demonic spirit in your life; a situation in which you need Christ to set you free.

Neanderthal: a brutish person.

Nearsighted: being shortsighted; a need to think futuristically or see down the road in your life.

Neck: pride; stubborn; strong willed; stiff-necked; rebellious; willingness; one who supports a leader or the one in authority.

Necklace: a person who is close to you; if it has a picture of someone it means your love for that person; a symbol of wise instruction and teaching from parents; a yoke around the neck; a bondage.

Needle (Eye of a Needle): God doing the possible against impossible odds as you pray.

Needle (Hypodermic): addiction, drug use.

Neighbor: often a literal call to pray for them; symbolically it means God's family; cursing your neighbor indicates not having common sense and having hatred in your heart for them.

Nest: security that is not real; one's home; God as a place of rest.

Nets: plans, traps or snares from physical or spiritual enemies; tools for winning the lost.

New: a new spiritual or emotional condition; new opportunities.

New Year: a new beginning; a fresh start; a fresh opportunity.

Newspaper: proclamation; prophetic utterance; bringing and revealing something to others; searching for information; staying knowledgeable.

Night: danger; an enemy; time of trial or difficulty; lack of understanding; living without Holy Spirit's guidance; spiritually lost.

Nightclub: foolish or sinful conduct.

Ninja: a black clad ninja indicates a special demonic envoy sent to kill, steal and destroy a person or ministry; a white ninja can indicate a godly person or angel to fight on your behalf.

Noah's Ark: God's promise of safety and provision.

Noise: an intrusive and irritating person or situation; a person who draws attention or distraction.

Noon: noonday brightness represents God's blessings and healing.

Noose: the trap awaiting the wicked; impending judgment.

Northern Army: the heavenly army.

North: refers to great power and authority that will come.

No Pants On: you are going to school and God is teaching you something that is going to make you spiritually reproductive.

Nose: a discerning spirit; being able to discern good or evil; one who gossips; someone who is snoopy or curious or you are wrongly sticking your nose into other people's business; pressing someone's nose indicates stirring up strife.

Nosebleed: strife; a need to strengthen your discernment.

Nosedive: unexpected loss of position, status or money.

Nostrils: large nostrils indicate a person is self-conscious about their appearance; a very snoopy person.

Notation: symbolic of your actions in life; if your life is not vir-

A to Z Christian Dream Symbols Dictionary

tuous the notes will scream or sound out of tune.

Numbness: being desensitized by life; feeling numb because of a traumatic event.

Nun: piety or dedication to God; hiding from people.

Nurse: caring; helping; an aid who brings one health in Christ; if you are the nurse it indicates your expert role in being used by God to assist someone.

Nursing/Breastfeeding: a call to breastfeed from God; feeding a desire either good or bad; helping young believers to grow in the faith.

Nuts (Food): the blessing and favor of God; receiving the best of the land.

Nuts and Bolts: able to take care of details.

O

Oak: great strength; deep spiritual roots.

Oar: without an oar in a boat means no progress; only one oar means going in circles.

Oasis: a place of refreshment and peace in God in a desert season of life.

Obesity: can mean low self-esteem; struggling with great well-fed fleshly desires.

Ocean: masses of people or a church; God's deep truths and judgments; if you are in a boat it can mean your journey in life; if swimming in the ocean it can mean you are exploring deep places in life or in the spirit; if tossed at sea it could mean immaturity; a stormy or raging ocean can symbolize groups or nations at war.

Occult: the demonic realm; can mean literal curses or spells are being cast on you.

Odor: can mean a curse; a demonic presence; a pleasant scent can mean goodness; a pleasing life or the presence of the Lord.

Office: symbolic of earthly or spiritual authority; a calling and gifting; can mean administration; your work; your performance or your function; co-workers; administrative details of a project.

Office Building: if prophetic ministry it could be you are being taken to a new office; something new or a new anointing may be coming.

Office Building (Repairing): it means you are being renewed or renovated; a refreshing is coming; a situation is changing.

Office Building (High Rise): can mean your status or level of calling; can mean where you are spiritually at the present or will be going depending on context.

Officer: leadership; a commission from God.

Ogre: wicked or abusive person; a demonic oppressor.

Oil: anointing; Holy Spirit; medicine; healing; joy; prosperity; grace and mercy of God.

Oil (Black Crude): soon coming abundant finances and gushing provision.

Oil Derrick: an ability to generate wealth.

Ointment: a good reputation; a soothing person; healing balm.

Old: your old life and ways; your old beliefs.

Old Age: indicates God's blessings.

Old or Former Church: can be a tradition or traditional church from your past.

Old Boyfriend or Girlfriend: usually stands for an old love verses love for God; we are in danger of going back to an old love and away from God; may be doing some old things that may lead us away from God and if we don't stop now we may not be able to stop from leaving the love of God.

Old Friends: same as ex-wife or old flame.

Old Homes: usually a time line drawing attention to a healing season.

Old Man: self or flesh; pre-Christian; spirit of wisdom.

Old Pets: old memories which can be bad or good depending on how you saw your old pet.

Olive/Olive Oil: adoption into God's family; oil of peace is coming; you or another have or will offer peace offerings.

Olive Tree: witness of God; power; Israel; believers;

Olive Tree (Green): a prosperous believer.

Olive branch: global symbol of peace; grafted-in believers.

Olympics: competing at a high level; performing well as a believer; needing endurance and stamina for a life test.

Omega: Christ always existing.

Onions: crying or tears over a situation or a person.

Onyx: God watching out for His people; God's protection.

Orchestra/Symphony: same as musical instruments

Orgy: dark sexual deviancy; influence or control from a spirit of perversion.

Orphan: having an orphan heart or life style; serving God out of performance or legalism instead of from love as a daughter or son; feeling emotionally or spiritually abandoned.

Orphanage: a call to minister, pray or support orphans.

Ostrich: poor common sense; heartlessness.

Ouija Board: playing around with demonic entities; under demonic control or influence.

Outer Space: feeling lost in the vastness of life or humanity; feeling separation; insight into the spirit realm; can also be the same as flying.

A to Z Christian Dream Symbols Dictionary

Oven: incubating new ideas or goals that require time and sometimes heat in your life; God's judgement; an angry heart.

Overslept: a chance of missing a divine appointment or advancement in the spiritual or natural realm.

Overtime: high pressure period in life in which you play a critical role.

Owl: demonic spirits disguised as spirit guides; an abomination.

Ox: slaughter; strength; increase.

Oyster: a producer; a home to hidden and sacred treasure; romance; love.

P

Paddle: discipline; if paddling a boat it indicates a lot of effort to make slow progress.

Pain: literal body pain; emotional pain to you or the body of Christ.

Paint/Painting: covering something up could be good or bad depending on the color and context of dream; creating a new image; renewing something in your life; revamping something or a situation; healing over old emotional wounds.

Painting (Picture): artistic gifting and value; the picture itself will give insight into its meaning.

Pale Horse: death.

Pallbearer: symbol of death and mortality; a friend carrying you through seasons of death or hardship or you carrying someone.

Palm (Hand): when opened to you it is an invitation and promise for care.

Palm reading: witchcraft, sorcery and divination.

Palm tree: symbolic of a person; peace; symbolic of flourishing; righteousness.

Panther: approaching or lurking evil.

Pants: if without pants it means you are in a vulnerable situation.

Paparazzi: fame or coming fame; may reveal idolatry; high respect of someone.

Parachute: bailing out of a situation or from a person; escaping or fleeing a situation or person; looking for safety and rescue during a crisis; if the parachute doesn't open properly or has holes it means what you are trusting to keep you safe in a life crisis won't protect you.

Parade: victory; success; can also mean needless pomp

Paralyzed: feeling paralyzed in your actual or spiritual life; someone trying to stop you from doing something or moving on in life; an enemy is trying to cripple you.

Paramedic: a help in time of an emergency; healing being close.

Parent: authority; Father God; an actual parent.

Park: a time to rest and relax; a time to enjoy creation; worship; tranquility; a temporary place; futility of living without Christ.

Parked Car: a ministry on the sideline or on hold; God could be telling you to take a sabbatical.

Parking Lots: short term people or short term ministry.

Parrot: a colorful character; someone gossiping or repeating what they hear.

Party: a time of celebration; it is ungodly celebration if it is wild, drugs or drinking.

Passenger In a Moving Vehicle: being someone's friend; going along with someone's decisions for your life; partners in ministry or in a move of God.

Passport: international travel; a call to missions.

Pastries: may represent gossip which is sweet to some.

Pasture: a peaceful life; rest; provision.

Patch: a need for Holy Spirit refill.

Path: one's path of life; your personal walk with God; if the path is level it represents walking in God's ways or directions in life for you; a hidden path can indicate an unseen option or choice in life.

Patience: God's favor; fruit of Holy Spirit.

Pawnshop: if you are pawning your things it indicates you are on a path of poverty or living under an orphan lifestyle.

Paycheck: the wages of one's lifestyle; financial reward; if the check says righteousness it means you are living a Godly life; if it says punishment it indicates you are living a wicked life.

Peace: proof of a God-centered thought life; feeling peace is a blessing from God; God's favor; Holy Spirit fruit.

Peaches: romantic desires; love.

Peacock: pride or showiness.

Pearl: object or person of value; an established truth of God; the Gospel; the value of people to God; the glory of heaven.

Pelican: distress; affliction.

Pen/Pencil: symbol of praise; a writing gift; a call to write a book; an ability to communicate; to make a permanent statement or reminder.

Penny: can be a symbol of poverty; a symbol of giving out of poverty.

Pentagram: satanic worship or occult practices.

People Watching You Go to the Bathroom and it Did Not Bother

A to Z Christian Dream Symbols Dictionary

You: the Lord is going to clean you up of things that are toxic to you in front of everyone and it is going to be okay because it didn't bother you in the dream so you won't be bothered by it in real life because it is a natural flow of God's work in people.

People Standing Off and Not Ministering When Needed: spiritual apathy.

Perfume: the glory and aroma of God; the fragrance of Holy Spirit; the prayers going up to God; joy and gladness of heart.

Peroxide: healing of emotional, spiritual or physical wounds.

Person Changes Appearance: you are in an unstable time in your life; can be demonic spirits such as shape shifter or skin walkers.

Pesticide: covering a problem with intercession; removing the tares of sin from your life.

Pestilence: God's judgment on wickedness.

Phantom: a demonic presence; can also indicate an old issue that is still lingering in your life.

Pharaoh: pride and a hard heart in someone who is in authority.

Phone: receiving a message from God; needing to talk to someone in your life; a call to hear God's voice; a call to dialog with God.

Photographer: holding onto memories which can be good or bad depending on the context or any pictures; keeping track or the memories of God's work in your life.

Physician: Christ; a pastor; if you are the physician it indicates you are a healer, comforter and counselor to others.

Picture: a way to bring attention to the person or image in the picture; something relating to images for you to keep in memory or to honor.

Picture Frames: a mind-set or mentality.

Golden Frames: a divine seal.

Old Frame: outdated thinking or beliefs.

Pigs: ungrateful people; mockers; scoffers; an unclean demonic spirit; messy or unclean living; spirit of religion; caged by one's mind-set; being phony and not trustworthy; selfish; hypocritical; there are things that are going wrong around you that are unclean or will lead to destruction; someone who is subtle and usually involved in real messy situations; a carrier of demons.

Pig snout: someone routing around in other people's business; if with a gold ring it can be a woman without discretion.

Pigeon: an offering for sin; a call to repentance.

Piggy Bank: laying up spiritual treasures a little at a time; faithful stewardship; using the little you have to help others.

Pillar: elders; mature believers; a symbol of responsibility; a main support to someone either spiritual or natural; foundational truths.

Pilot: piloting a plane indicates a fast paced ministry or lifestyle; piloting a commercial jetliner indicates leadership in an international ministry or company.

Pimple/Acne: a situation that needs to come to a head to find healing.

Pinion: God's faithfulness and protection.

Pioneers: leadership; trailblazers; the opposite of a settler.

Pirate: an outcast; a thieving spirit sent to steal your finances, your dreams or destiny.

A to Z Christian Dream Symbols Dictionary

Pirate Flag: an impending attack in your life or the life of another.

Pistol: being spiritually armed for a natural or demonic fight; the bullets are symbolic of your words.

Pit: an enticement; a trap; a hole on your life pathway to be avoided.

Pitcher (Container): the container of Holy Spirit wine.

Pitcher (Baseball): a place of great responsibility; a place of high pressure; a place of great victory.

Pizza: quick spiritual food to get you through a situation; a frozen pizza indicates being spiritually unprepared.

Places You Have Been With Many Relatives: can be harassment; bloodline curses or blessings; inheritances; can mean the family environment in a church makes you feel like home.

Plague: God's judgment upon wickedness.

Planting: sowing and reaping something that can be bad or good depending on what was planted; if sowing fruit or vegetable seeds it indicates God's blessings.

Plants (Vines): family and children; reaping your actions; if the plants are withered it indicates a lack of true spiritual life.

Plastic: flexibility; pliable; weak and not strong.

Plate (/Platter): having a lot on your plate to do; servanthood.

Platoon: united in purpose; a united group of praying believers in spiritual warfare.

Play/Playing: enjoying life; the game of life; not serious about life; competition; contention; spiritual warfare.

Playground: a time or place to be childlike; a call to maturity.

Playing Field: contested territory.

Plaza (Open Area): crying out or bringing a message to people.

Plow: new ground in life or ministry to break into; faithful; a difficult or hard ministry situation; preparing the heart to receive from God or His Word; breaking through ground hardened by sin.

Plumbing: opening a channel to people or God; trying to unclog a channel to people or God.

Plumb line: lining up with the truth.

Plumbing (Pipes): the flow of life; there is an obstruction in your life if pipes are clogged or crooked.

Poison: wicked activities; false beliefs; evil things or people in your life; lying; wicked or poison words; can also be life killing grief.

Poker (Card Game): taking risks; a good hand indicates you have an advantage in a situation; if you have a poor hand it means you need to make peace with your opponent.

Polar Bear: a large problem; a nasty or dangerous person or situation.

Police/Cop: spiritual authority; having to enforce something; having power to enforce something either good or bad; a pastor; elders; angels or demons; bosses or leaders.

Polishing: preparation and refinement; paying attention to excellence in one's work.

Pollution: nation's wickedness; sin in one's life.

Polygraph Machine: indicates a need to be truthful in a situation.

Pomegranates: God's sweetness; beauty; ministry.

Pompous: a person without understanding of God.

Pond or Pool: a small place where people gather together; the work place; a club; a school; a church; if dirty it means people are gathering for wickedness.

Pool Hall: people trying to scam or deceive you.

Porch: being open to others; exhibition; easily seen or displayed.

Porcupine: a prickly person or situation; a worrisome situation or person.

Pornography: spirit of perversion controlling you; in contact with a sexually perverse person.

Port (Harbor): can indicate you are running from God's call on your life; you are about to embark on international ministry or travel.

Port-a-Potty: bad jokes; bathroom humor; a dirty or potty mouth.

Possession: a feeling of spiritual possession indicates demonic control in your life.

Postage Stamp: a seal of authority; authorization; being empowered; being ready to be sent out in ministry; provision for sending.

Postman: a messenger; the contents of the letter may be a reminder to pray over any good or bad news you receive in life.

Post Mortem: examining what is happening or has happened; giving testimony.

Pot (Container): a person; tradition.

Pot (Marijuana): see drugs.

Pot Hole: being stuck or hitting a rocky path in your life journey.

Potter's Wheel: molded or fashioned by God.

Pottery: a Godly vessel; if broken it means you have lost your spiritual strength and ability to carry the things of God to others.

Praise: singing to the Lord indicates a Godly person.

Prayer: a call to prayer; while asleep it proves our spirit never sleeps.

Preacher/Clergy: religion; Jesus the Great Pastor and Shepherd; a literal pastor; the character of the preacher can be bad or good depending on the context.

Pregnancy: conceiving an idea and waiting through its gestation and delivery; final stages of a trial or test; a circumstance or preparation time; a wilderness time; a literal pregnancy.

Prescription: instructions for physical, emotional or spiritual healing in your life.

Preservatives: jars filled with jams and jellies indicates God's love, kindness, truth and preservation of you in life.

Pressure: you are under pressure to perform or accomplish a task; God's correction and discipline; can also be a demonic hindrance in your life if it is a dark dream or nightmare.

Pressure cooker: feeling in a pressure cooker of life or in a relationship.

Prince: Christ; a prince of a person; a dark prince means a demonic principality or satan.

A to Z Christian Dream Symbols Dictionary

Princess: a royal position of a woman believer; can also symbolize a difficult woman.

Principal: position of authority; demonic principality or territorial spirit over a region or group.

Prison/Dungeon: not having any hope for the future; bondages or restrictions placed on you; feeling you are imprisoned in life.

Prisoner: a lost person; emotional captivity; feeling bound by depression, anxiety, sinful habits or addictions; being taken captive by satan or the demonic realm.

Prophet: God's voice to you so pay attention to precisely what is said.

Prostitute: a path of death.

Pruning: season of God removing things from you to promote growth.

Psychic (Mediums): an evil spirit trying to counsel you in a dream.

Pulpit: a call to preach or teach.

Puppet/Marionette: being controlled by a demonic spirit or other people.

Purse/Wallet: wealth or finances; personal identity; something precious and valuable; if full it is ample provision for your calling or purpose; if empty it means bankrupt in spirit or identity.

Pyramid: reaching for worldly goals rather than Godly Goals; can stand for occult or false gods.

Python: see snakes.

Q-R

Q-tip: a need to clean out one's ears and listen to wisdom and God.

Quacking: a complaining person; having harsh or annoying speech.

Quadruplets: double portion— a double double.

Quail: God's creative provision in a desert time in your life.

Quarterback: leadership under pressure; great responsibility.

Quarters: represents 1/4 of something; 1/4 of a year.

Queen: high status in a social group; the Queen of Heaven; an evil focus of worship or idolatry.

Queen Bee: an aggressive or domineering woman; a highly productive person.

Question Marks: questions that you need answers for in your life.

Quicksand: an emotional sinking that can kill you physically, emotionally or spiritually; caught in the clutches of an addiction, unhealthy habit or sin.

Quiver: the womb; many actual or spiritual children.

Quiz: a short season or period of time in which you are tested; a time of endurance; running the race of life.

Rabbits: a pagan symbol of fertility; a demon manifesting as

A to Z Christian Dream Symbols Dictionary

spirit guide with a human body and a rabbit head; evil spirits; something capable of multiplication either good or bad depending on context; sexual torment; a destructive person or action.

Rabbit Foot: false hope; worldly luck; trusting in something other than God.

Raccoon: a person prone to foolish behavior or mischief; a troublesome person who is a pest.

Race: your journey in life; a competitive spirit; a fast paced lifestyle.

Radio: a person who continuously broadcasts their views; communication in the spirit realm either good or bad; a prophetic utterance; proclaiming the gospel; a nuisance; God calling you to minister through means of radio.

Raft: safety on the troubled seas of life; safety in time of trouble; feeling without purpose or direction; a lifesaving situation.

Rags: poverty; lack; humility; dead works.

Railroad Track: you are on track with God; having a one track mind; tradition; unchanging habit; stubborn; unyielding; not teachable; caution; danger.

Rain: blessings; God's Word; a soft rain is the peaceful presence of Holy Spirit, flourishing and prosperity; a downpour can indicate a coming outpouring of the Spirit; if a hard rain it can the mean the storms of life, a hindrance, a trial or disappointment; if a drought it can mean a lack of blessings or an absence of God's manifest presence.

Rainbows: faithfulness; love; a sign of God's covenant; a sign of natural agreement or promise; God will keep His promises to you.

Raisin: intercession; revival; peace offering.

Raisin Cake: love; refreshing.

Ram: God's provision when the time of testing has passed; occult or satanic.

Rape: being violated emotionally or spiritually without consent by force; being sexually assaulted in a dream is a demonic spirit attacking you; God wanting to heal an actual rape.

Rapist: the demonic realm trying to take something from you without consent.

Rapids: fast paced out-of-control circumstances; a fast moving change or advancement in your life; a fast growing ministry.

Rapture: a call to salvation or prayer for the lost; a call to be caught up with God.

Rat: a person with low character, morals and ethics; garbage or sin in someone's life; larger or more authoritative demonic attacks that feed off of garbage in your life because you gave them permission to be there by allowing the garbage; an ungodly passion or desire; see mice.

Rattle Snake: see snakes.

Ravens: a messenger; provision; can be a demonic spirit depending on the context; a scavenger in your life.

Raw Meat: a need for diligence and preparation; eating raw meat can mean laziness; an unfinished business or task.

Razor: lies, deceit and destruction; a clean break from circumstances, sin or a habit.

Reap/Reaping: a time of harvest; a reward for effort either good or bad.

Rearview Mirror: focusing on the past or past hurts; not moving forward.

Recliner: peaceful; relaxing; rest.

A to Z Christian Dream Symbols Dictionary

Red Cross: helping without expecting anything in return; salvation and Christ's sacrifice of His life; a believer's service.

Red Eyes: red-eyed entities are demonic; can also indicate fatigue or drinking alcohol.

Red Horse: war.

Red Tape: a long and tedious process in achieving a goal; having to jump through numerous hoops to get something accomplished or be promoted.

Reed: a fear of people's perceptions and opinions; weakness either natural or spiritual; being or feeling too weak to be relied on.

Referee: a mediator or advocate; Christ; a person of authority; the literal person in the dream.

Reflection: seeing yourself in mirror or water represents seeing into your heart; reveals how you perceive your spiritual image.

Refrigerator: the place where heart issues are kept; stored up thoughts; storing up spiritual food for a right time; if spoiled food it means you harbor a grudge or unclean thoughts and desires.

Refuge: a place of protection; safety; security.

Reins: a need to rein yourself or someone else in; someone trying to rein you in; a means of control or restraint.

Relatives: your current living conditions; family; teamwork; if they are dead relatives it can be showing you the root of generational blessings or curses in your life.

Relay Race: working as a team to accomplish a goal or ministry; continuing another's ministry.

Remote Control: control over an aspect in your life or in another; jezebel spirit in you or another.

139

Rending: repentance; disagreement; to tear apart is a sign of anger, grief or sorrow.

Reporter: searching for information for other's benefit or to do them harm.

Reptile: a demonic spirit.

Reservoir: storing up spiritual food and strength; a waterless reservoir is putting your trust in someone other than God.

Resistance: human or demonic resistance; someone resisting what you are trying to do; someone resisting your message.

Restaurant: a place of choice regarding the spiritual food you need; a place where the five-fold ministry is taught and in operation; a place where spiritual food is prepared; a church.

Resting: no activity; ministering out of rest in God.

Resurrection: coming to life where there was death either physically, spiritually or emotionally.

Resuscitate: your life; a situation or desire brought back to life.

Reunion: unity; reuniting with God and the things of God; reuniting with people.

Revolver: armed with the Word of God.

Rhinestones: artificiality; phoniness; insincerity or deceit.

Rib: a relationship between a man and his wife; united or as one in purpose and belief.

Ribbon: can be reminders; depends on color and what it is tied on to; on a heart shaped place it is probably to remind you of issues of the heart; to love someone; to do something for someone; praise; worship; celebration; reward.

Riches: God's financial security; spiritual riches in Christ.

Riddle: someone telling or reading riddles is God wanting you to search His mysteries out.

Riding in a Chariot: God is taking you on a spiritual journey; God has a celestial destiny and something for you to accomplish; chariots represent something you or someone is going to accomplish; if someone is in it with you it means they will accomplish it with you.

Riding a White Horse: power and purity; something God has for you that has purity and the purposes of God and it involves power; horses always represent either good or bad power.

Rifle: someone attacking with precisely aimed words; being armed with the Word of God against the enemy.

Right: authority; power; natural inclinations; what you can do naturally.

Right Turn: natural changes; a turn toward wisdom.

Ring: favor; affirmation; a never ending situation; something unchanging and not interrupted; a unity of purpose in a place; a covenant relationship; God's approval or authority; a symbol of our covenant with God.

Ring (Engagement): promise; sign of commitment.

Ring (as Jewelry): Vanity; worldliness.

Ring (Wedding): marriage between man and woman; symbolizes our marriage to Jesus.

River: life's journey; a refreshing time; peace like a river; a clean life; living water; a movement of God; the flow of Holy Spirit; an obstacle in your life; a trial.

Deep River: deep things of God.

Dangerous Currents: difficulty in moving in the flow of the Spirit; turmoil and stress.

Dried Up River: danger ahead; a lack of God's presence; traditions or legalism; empty of Spiritual power.

Muddy River: operating in mixtures of flesh and spirit.

Peaceful River: God's blessings.

Roaches: an unclean demonic spirit or person; someone or something that can cause and thrive on sin.

Roads: direction for one's life path; choices to make.

Road (Bumpy): a rough period in life.

Road (Smooth): God's intervention on your behalf.

Roadblock: something stopping you from your life's journey, destiny, desire or goal.

Road Signs: a call to follow the sign's message of stop, change direction, go slow or yield.

Yield Sign: a need or call to submission.

Roadrunner: speed; swiftness.

Roaring: hearing the roar of an animal is a warning of impending danger; feeling or being a defenseless victim.

Robber: an evil person; demonic activity in one's life; an adulterer.

Robe: relaxation; wealth and authority; if wearing a gold, blue, purple or scarlet it robe means holiness, glory and beauty; if wearing a white robe it means righteousness; if the robe is spotted it means sin in your life.

Robots: acting without any conscious; being controlled by another or a demonic spirit.

Rock: Jesus Christ; solid foundations; a place of refuge and safety; an obstacle or stumbling block.

A to Z Christian Dream Symbols Dictionary

Rocket: a ministry or person with great power or potential for deep things of the Spirit; a ministry capable of quick take-off and great speed in growth or outreach; a quick and sudden move in an area of your life which can be good or bad depending on circumstances.

Rocking: a reflective time; you are rocking back and forth in making a decision.

Rocking Chair: intercession; reflection; old age; meditation; recollection; prayer; relaxation.

Rod: Word's of Christ; a staff or scepter of authority; to guard someone or something; being disciplined or having to discipline another depending on context.

Roll Bar: safety from troubles or disasters; able to rise back up unhurt under hurtful situations.

Roller Coasters: emotional or spiritual instability in life; if it is a family member it can mean they don't know how to get themselves or others out of a particular situation or problem; the swings of seasons or moods in one's life; a situation or circumstance that moves up and down; an up and down Christian life; a thrilling and fun life.

Roller Skates: a skillful walk with God; making speedy progress in a spiritual or emotional situation; a fast moving but possibly dangerous situation or ministry.

Roof: a spiritual covering for your household; protection in life's storms; revelation from above; thinking; meditation; negatively it can be something in your life preventing you from connecting with God; a leaking or damaged roof means idleness and laziness.

Rooms: chapters in your life; rooms filled with good things means a person with knowledge and wisdom; a dirty room indi-

143

cates a person's unclean lifestyle.

Rooster: a wakeup call; denial of Jesus; pride; a noisy person.

Roots: can indicate a righteous person; if it has fruit it indicate a good person; symbolic of being firmly planted; a history or origin of a thing or people; if the root is dry it means evil; roots of sin and iniquity.

Rope/Cord: bound in sin or in a situation; a covenant; a triple braided cord symbolizes power in unity.

Rosary: piety, life of prayer; legalism or works based salvation or relationship with God; a religious spirit.

Roses: great beauty and value; a symbol of love; healing; our relationship with Jesus; Jesus the Rose of Sharon.

Rotting Fruit: a sign of bad choices in life.

Roulette: hoping for an unlikely outcome in a situation; taking chances in the wheel of life.

Round (Shape): never ending, favor, love, mercy; feeling you are in a never ending situation.

Row Boat: a ministry that intervenes for others; feeling you are going through life with a lot of effort; a slow moving or growing ministry; offering earnest prayer.

Rowing: continually working at something; laboring in the spirt; traveling in the Spirit; hard work or hard work under oppression; difficulty in getting through a circumstance..

Rubbing: someone rubbing you indicates sensuousness or an unwanted advance from another person; someone is rubbing you the wrong way.

Rubble: calamity; sin or garbage in one's life.

Rubies: something of great value in life; something in your life on display.

A to Z Christian Dream Symbols Dictionary

Rug: trying to cover up flaws or something in your life; protection; to soften.

Rugby: playing at the game of life.

Ruler/Tape Measure: trying to measure up; feeling you measure up or don't measure up.

Running: you are doing well in life; your race or journey in life; hard work; trying to catch up with something or someone.

Running with a Leg that won't straighten out: something in the spirit that is not fully operating in you or another yet; a part of your life you have not yet given over to the Lord so you go about doing God's work but are only limping along; it can also mean a church that does not believe in prophetic ministry or all of the 5 fold offices are not functioning effectively.

Running in Slow Motion: same as limping.

Rust: old thoughts or beliefs; feeling you are tarnished or blemished; needing practice or cleansing; temporal things; earthly riches.

145

S

Sackcloth: mourning; fasting; a call to repentance and prayer.

Sacrifice: to lay down one's life for another; you have something in you to cover up or wash away.

Safe: being kept safe physically, emotionally or spiritually; a place of safety.

Sails: empowered by Holy Spirit; empowered by prophecy.

Salesman: a persuasive person; someone able to motivate others to action; an evangelist.

Salmon: having to swim upstream or going against the flow which can be bad or good depending on the context.

Salt: a believer's character; believers as salt of the earth; something or someone that adds value; one who preserves or purifies; making a lasting impression or result; graceful speech; healing water.

Salt Flats: desolation; abandonment; feeling all alone.

Salt Pit: desolation and destruction.

Salt Water: adding flavor to a situation; to cleanse a situation.

Same Person as Two People: someone doing something to another person that is usually very self-destructive; you are being involved in another's destruction; positively it can mean you are being involved in building someone up.

A to Z Christian Dream Symbols Dictionary

Same People Have Same Dream: in the mouth of two or three witnesses everything is established.

Sanctuary: a sacred place, a refuge; a place of immunity or rest; a place set apart for prayer or intimacy with God.

Sand: numerous seeds; many promises; a symbol of a long life; symbolic of a work of flesh; not suitable for a spiritual foundation.

Sandals: spreading the good news.

Sandstorm: having great trials or troubles in life or ones are coming.

Sap: being full of life; a person who feels he is a sap.

Sapphire: something of high value and beauty.

Satan: indicating demonic activity in your life that you can rebuke in the name of Jesus.

Saw: God's power to cut or tear down; cutting sin out of your life.

Scabs: afflictions; an emotional wound is healing but is not to be picked at.

Scaffolding: a work in progress; being a support to someone or a ministry.

Scale (Reptile): great pride; a hard shelled person.

Scales: being weighed in the balance; trying to balance situations in your life; judging the worth or value of a person or object.

Scars: past emotional wounds and hurts; a need for faith in Jesus.

Scarecrow: fear; someone attempting to bring fear into your life; a demonic spirit of fear; you may be putting your faith in the wrong place or something that is unable to help.

Scenes (Different): sometimes we may have more than one dream in a night but it is often the same dream with more than one scene; they are all about one thing, but different facets and perspectives of the same issue.

Scepter: a ministry office; a staff of authority or sovereignty.

School: a training period; a time or place of teaching in your life; a teaching ministry; a time or place for getting tools for life; retaking tests in life that you have failed; tests you have passed; missing tests because of interruptions and distractions that caused you to fail; a grade level shows difficulty of tests you are facing in life.

School Classroom: a spiritual training place; a place of teaching; a ministry with a teaching anointing.

Scissors: cutting or pruning ungodly things out of your life or a need to do so; cutting through what isn't real.

Scorpion: evil spirit; poisonous person; someone wanting to harm you; black scorpion means black magic & evil; white scorpion can mean someone is using white magic which is still evil.

Scream: you try to scream but only a whisper comes out means there are circumstances in your life that are hindering or preventing prayer.
Screws: a need to get something together in your life; a need to tighten up an area of your life.

Scroll: written commands; precepts; a specific word or commission from God; you need to pay attention to what is written.

Sea: a great multitude of people; nations of the world; being unsettled as the mark of the sea; a method or plan by which to reach the nations; a great obstacle.

Sea Coast: a transitional phase; a borderland situation.

A to Z Christian Dream Symbols Dictionary

Sea of Glass: a peaceful and clear situation; a symbol of revelation; stillness; transparency.

Sea Monster: a powerful human or demonic attack on you.

Seal: confirmation; authenticity or a guarantee from God or a person; God's mark of approval or belonging; a mark of evil.

Séance: someone with occult ties may be trying to influence your life; if you are participating in a séance it is a warning that you have become involved in the occult.

Seat: a person's social rank; a right to occupy a certain position in a group; a power base; ruler-ship; authority; coming to rest; a place of mercy.

Seat Belt: protection from people or the demonic, especially in ministry.

Secretary: a helper; assistants in dreams may be angels; a gate-keeper to information or people of authority.

Security Guard: often an angel; a protector with authority and power.

Sediment: something in your life is worthless; being undisturbed.

Seed: children; the Word of God; a promise; a person or situation capable of giving rise to many greater things either good or bad; stewarding resources; an investment to be tended.

Seeing Creation: you or someone is entering a time of great creativity where God is going to unfold His plan before you.

Self Portrait: self-examination.

Selling: if selling grain it indicates a blessing from God; person refusing to sell you something that you need is symbolic of a hated person.

149

Sepulcher: your old life in the grave; something you thought was dead will resurrect to life either good or bad depending on the context.

Serial Killer: a demon who has been sent to try to take your physical or spiritual life.

Serpent: a symbol of satan; kingdoms of the world; an accursed thing; a cunning person; gossip; persecution; a spirit of divination.

Sewage: a good appearance but carrying waste within; sewage in your life that is defiling you.

Sewer: a dirty environment; can mean God is flushing garbage out of your life.

Sewing Clothes: an industrious person; a good wife; able to put things together in a situation or ministry; mending situations or relationships; union; counseling.

Sewing Machine: doing good deeds towards others; sowing the Word.

Sexual Dreams: may reveal a spirit of lust; same sex or opposite sex can be flushing dreams; if dreaming of a past relationship you need to break soul ties in prayer.

Sexual Encounter Dreams: may be telling us we are going back to an old way or an old love that is trying to take the place of the Lord; soulish desires; you want to be intimate with another person's gifts; if having sexual intercourse it can be a result of having contact with someone with a spirit of perversion.

Sex with Old Lover: could be cleansing dream; can mean you desire your old life.

Shack: a flimsy life; not trusting God.

A to Z Christian Dream Symbols Dictionary

Shackles: affliction; bondage; oppression; feeling you are shackled in life or in ministry.

Shade: a reprieve from hard work; a reprieve from spiritual battle; protection.

Shadow: reflection of a person or situation; a spiritual cover; covered by God; place of safety & security; if only partially illuminated it means a poor resemblance of something else; a delusion or imitation of the real; being imperfect or lacking real substance; a spirit of death; demons.

Shaking: indicates fear; God is shaking out the useless things in your life.

Shaking Hands: symbolizes agreement; friendship.

Shampoo/Conditioner: a need for cleansing and conditioning of your heart; a softening heart or a need for softening; cleansing from under wrong authority.

Shark: a hidden demonic predator or a person with the ability to cause you great harm; a need to pray for protection; represents the opposite of peace; fear; an enemy trying to devour you or your ministry.

Shattered Cup: can mean ruin and destruction; unable or unfit to carry the anointing.

Shaving: shaving your legs or face may indicate a desire to appear acceptable to others; cutting yourself while shaving indicates anxiety associated with trying to put on a good appearance.

Shawl: being covered by God or someone in authority; anointing.

Sheep: believers; children of the Great Shepherd.

151

Sheepdog: call to evangelism; rounding up the lost.

Sheets: clean and fragrant bed sheets indicate virtuous living; dirty bed sheets indicate the opposite

Shelter: a place of protection from your enemies and pitfalls in life; a refuge God provides from spiritual enemies and people who spread strife.

Shelves: there may be things you need to put on a shelf for a season.

Shepherd: Jesus; a leader of something either good or bad; an ability to separate good teaching from bad teaching, may be a literal leader to pray for; may be a call to ministry or call to minister to someone.

Sheriff: a pastor or teacher; someone who will keep you accountable for your actions or belief.

Shield: your faith to extinguish demonic attacks; God's faithfulness to His servants; a small shield is symbolic of God's arsenal of weapons against His enemies.

Shining Face: God's blessings.

Shirt: one's personal spiritual covering; sacrificial giving as in giving the shirt off your back.

Shoes: symbolizes a servant; a journey; a readiness to spread the gospel; knowledge of the Word of God; walking in peace.

Boots: equipped for spiritual warfare.

Shoes Do Not Fit: walking in what you are not called for.

Giving Away Shoes: equipping others; blessing others.

High Heels: seduction; uncomfortable with what you are doing.

In Need of Shoes: not dwelling in God's Word; in need of comfort or protection.

New Shoes: getting new understanding of the gospel or God's Word; a fresh mandate from God; a new equipping for a new calling.

Putting On Shoes: preparation for a journey physically or spiritually.

Slippers: being too comfortable in life; not taking risks in ministry.

Snowshoes: faith; walking in the Spirit; supported by faith in the Word of God.

Taking off Shoes: honoring God; ministering to the Lord.

Taking Another's Shoes Off: showing respect and humility.

Tennis Shoes: spiritual gifting; running the race of life.

Shopping: choices and selections to be made in life or a circumstance.

Shopping Cart: what is in the cart is what to focus on; food = spiritual food, etc.

Shopping Center/Market Place: a ministry with multi-faceted gifting; a place of choices that may lead to not being single-minded; the various methods of the enemy strategies.

Short: being short is feeling unimportant or insignificant; if seeing others shorter than you it means you feel superior to others or another person.

Shoulder/s: responsibility; authority; shouldering burdens; government.

Bare Female Shoulders: enticement.

Broad Shoulders: capable of handling much responsibility.

Drooped Shoulders: defeated attitude; overworked; overtired and burned out.

Dislocated shoulder: calamity; unable to perform a task or handle a situation.

Shove: to push someone indicates aggression, rage and anger.

Shovel: hard work or a hard worker; digging up something in order to smear someone; digging up nuggets from God's Word; digging for good things in others.

Shower: being in a shower or seeing someone shower is a symbol of exposure or intimacy; can also indicate perversion or a perverse spirit.

Shrine: idol worship.

Sick: may indicate a sinful lifestyle or environment that is bad for you.

Sickle: harvest or harvesting for souls; evangelism; coming into your destiny; reaping the Word of God; reaping what you have sown.

Siege Works: being involved in a spiritual battle.

Sieve: separating the impure from the pure; a trial or testing; feeling things are slipping by you.

Sign: a witness of something; to foreshadow something or an event; to draw attention to a person, place or circumstance.

Crossroads/Intersection: a time or place for decision; a time for changing directions in your life.

Stop Sign: stop and pray for guidance; a call to stop a bad habit or sin in your life.

Yield Sign: a sign of submission; a time to submit to someone.

Signaling: winking, pointing and signaling others with your hands or feet can indicate an underhanded person.

Signet Ring: God's approval and authority; belonging to God or another which can be good or bad depending on the context.

Signature: commitment; responsibility; ownership.

Signs: looking for or needing directions in life.

Silence: a wise person.

Silver: pure words and truth; can also mean a high quality ministry; a symbol of redemption; understanding; insight; knowledge; testing; refining; an object or person of valor; worldly knowledge; betrayal; a furnace of affliction.

Silver Cord: symbolizes a person's spinal cord, hence his strength.

Simulator: being trained to run the race of life; training before ministry.

Singing: the words of the song equals a message from God; rejoicing; thankfulness to God; heart overflow.

Sinking: dying; disaster; overwhelming trouble in life; emotional despair; failing ministry or business.

Sirens: a warning that a battle is coming; a call to pray and trust for victory.

Sister: wisdom; one's actual sister or similar qualities in you or someone else; a sister in Jesus Christ; a dear friend.

Sister-in -law: the same as sister; one's actual sister-in -law or a person with similar qualities; a Christian in another fellowship; a relationship without much depth.

Sitting: a place of rest; a time out from ministry; a place of authority; a position of power; the throne of God; the seat of satan.

Skating: enjoying life.

Skeleton: death to a dream or death to an area of sin in your life; if kissing a skeleton it means you hate wisdom and love death.

Skiing: stepping out in faith; the power of faith; smooth riding in God's provision; making rapid process.

Skins: a covering.

Skipping: childlike behavior; being carefree; negatively it can mean avoiding responsibility.

Skirt: seeing someone's skirt lifted indicates public humiliation; having weaknesses exposed.

Skull/Crossbones: someone in the occult; death; someone opposing Christ's message.

Sky: God's presence; things related to God or high things of the Spirit; a dark sky means trouble; a clear sky means peace; a red sky means judgment or war; a purple sky can indicate the second coming of Jesus; can also mean witness and faithfulness.

Skydiving: free fall in life; freedom with risks; if you have a parachute it means safe landing; if the chute won't open or is ripped it means you are putting your hopes in something that is worthless or won't help you.

Skyscraper: revelation; a ministry or person with a built up structure to function on a multilevel; a church or person with prophetic gifted-ness; a high level of spiritual experience.

Slam Dunk: performing well in life; easy life or ministry.

Slap: either you have contempt for another or someone has contempt for you.

A to Z Christian Dream Symbols Dictionary

Slaughter House: being butchered emotionally or physically by someone.

Slavery: indicates oppression; bondage; sin.

Sled: a call to expedient prayers during wartime.

Sleeping: rest from life troubles; being overtaken; not being aware of problems; hiding from life; laziness; in danger; out of control; a need for spiritual awakening.

Overslept: in danger of missing a divine appointment.

Sleeping Bag: travel; emotional or spiritual homelessness; not having a permanent home.

Slingshot: you are fighting spiritual or physical enemies.

Slippery Path: you are heading down a slippery path of sin; judgment upon the wicked; calamity and punishment for wicked behavior.

Slipping: feeling you are slipping in your spiritual walk; being envious of wicked and arrogant people.

Slithering: indicates demonic influences in the person's life.

Smelter: being tested in order to purify.

Smile: a sign of friendliness; an act of kindness; agreement.

Smiling: a sign of friendship or a joyous heart; a seductive action.

Smoke: an irritating and lazy servant; indicates how quickly the wicked vanish from their lofty position; praise and worship; the manifested glory of God; prayers of the saints; hindrances.

Smoking: an addictive behavior or lifestyle.

Smooth Tongue: adultery; seductress; an untrustworthy person.

157

Snail: a wicked person; slowness; feeling your Christian growth is going at a snail's pace.

Snake Charmer: needing to be skillful, cautious and wise around certain people.

Snakes: all snakes represent spiritual or human enemies; lying spirits; spirits of confusion; satan, alcohol; wine; backbiting; gossip; long tales; slander; divination; false accusations; false prophecies; depending on the length of the snake someone is telling a big or a little tale about you; a large number of small snakes usually means many gossips that are gossiping.

Adders: spiritual or physical enemies; something small but deadly; someone or something that has the power to paralyze you.

Cobra: a wicked person; a demon; a paralyzing or deadly person or situation; a venomous person; evil words that can spread far.

King Cobra: a paralyzing demonic spirit.

Vipers: deadly gossip or persecution; a malignant or spiteful person.

Flying snake: a false religious spirit; a deadly and difficult to kill problem.

Anaconda: a crushing problem; something or someone squeezing the life out of you or out of a ministry; anxiety or depression.

Boa Constrictor: depression; anxiety; demonic attacker; someone or something is squeezing the life out of you either emotionally or spiritually.

Rattle Snake: evil words against you; strife; a warning that someone will attack you if you continue to bother, irritate or

A to Z Christian Dream Symbols Dictionary

provoke them.

Moccasin: human or spiritual enemies that will attack without provocation.

Snake on a Pole: an emblem of Jesus.

Python: a spirit of divination; witchcraft; a fierce or violent person; someone constricting your spiritual life; a large demonic spirit crushing you with depression, anxiety or hopelessness.

Flying Snake/Serpent: a deadly or hard to kill persistent enemy.

Grass Snake: a harmless human or spiritual pest.

Fangs: dangerous actions or poisonous words coming against you or another.

Snare: trap; fear of man; brought into bondage.

Snow: a symbol of peace, calm, serenity, purity and cleanness; a call to war in prayer; snow heralds war; covers sin; the favor of God; means totally pure if white, but if dirty snow it means no longer pure; a blizzard means blindness in a situation or resistance in life.

Soap: spiritual cleansing; forgiveness; interceding for others.

Soccer: the game of life; a contest of wills against another group of people.

Socks: reflective of the state of one's heart as fertile ground for God's Word; peace.

Dirty/Worn Socks: a blemished heart and walk before God.

White Socks: an unblemished heart and walk before God.

Soldier: spiritual warfare; a part of God's army or satan's army; a call for more prayers; fasting and worship; a period of trial or persecution.

Son: a child of God; a ministry or gifting from God; one's actual son or someone with similar traits.

Soft Drink: a refreshing time in life.
Soldier: a believer in God' army.

Soil: the condition of a person's heart.

Soot: desolation; a curse; depravation.

Sorcerer: demonic influence or control.

Sore: unconfessed sin in one's life; can be emotional injuries or pain caused by another that has not healed.

Soul Ties: generally unholy and need to be broken or severed.

Soulish Dream: if it brings peace it is probably the Lord saying He is going to give you the desires of your heart.

Sour: sour fruit or sour taste indicates sin or taking the wrong action; corruption; a sour disposition; sour words.

South: a place of peace; a source of refreshment; a natural inclination to do something.

Sowing: planning for the future either good or bad; spreading the Word of God.

Space: separation or feeling separated.

Spaceship: a speedy departure; leaving a job, position or location for another very quickly.

Spanking: discipline or punishment.

Sparkplug: igniting spiritual desires; igniting life in others.

Speaking: revealing the secrets of your heart.

Spear: may represent a weapon against God's enemies; a spear tip can indicate the point of the enemies attack; the strategy

God is going to give you for a problem; good words; the Word of God; evil words or curses.

Sphere: a person's area of influence; the color will give more information.

Spiders: lies and confusion; a web of deceit; an evil spirit that works by entrapping people, false doctrine; deception; the occult; sin; temptation; someone in the occult trying to harm you, but knowing can be good because then you can attack, squash or stop it.

Spider Web: a trap made of lies and confusing information.

Spiral: a spiral staircase or mountain path indicates progressively moving up or down in life from one area to another.

Spirit Guide: demonic spirit posing as a guide to the supernatural; spirit guides usually manifest in dreams as a talking person or animal; sometimes demons pose as a dead relative.

Spit: utter contempt for someone or something.

Splinter: angry at others over minor things.

Spoon: ability to feed yourself or others spiritually.

Sports: indicates the game of life.

Spot: a fault; a character blemish; feeling contamination; if without spot it means a glorious church.

Spring Time: new beginnings and new life.

Spring Rain: the presence of God.

Sprinkling: spiritual change by washing away dirt in your life; cleansing; purifying; consecrating.

Springs of Water: blessings of the Lord; person's heart; Holy Spirit in you; if clear water it is purity of speech; if dirty it means deceit.

Spy: people who influence the opinions of other believers over issues of ministry direction; witches sent in to destroy churches.

Square: tradition; a mind-set that is worldly and blind to truth.

Squatters: evil spirits in possession of something or someone without any authority to be there.

Stadium: someone or a ministry that has tremendous impact.

Staff: someone coming along side to give strength or help; pastoral ministry; the tools of a shepherd; the power of old age.

Staggering: becoming weak in faith; being led away from the truth by a spirit of distortion; being drunk from alcohol.

Stagnant Water: spiritual apathy; feeling stuck in life.

Stairs or Stairways: step by step progression towards a goal in life; a means of bringing about changes or transition, taking you to a higher or lower place in life or prayer, depending if you are going up or down.

Downstairs: demolition; backsliding; failure.

Guardrail: safety; precaution; a warning to be careful.

Standard: a banner or military standard is a sign that can be good or bad depending on the context or what is written on the banner

Standing: your firmness in faith; committed to a belief; a task not finished.

Standing Straight: no crookedness in you and you are going in the correct direction; standing against the devil and evil; standing against temptation.

Standing Off to the Side Not Doing Anything: you are not doing something you are supposed to be doing; spiritual apathy;

A to Z Christian Dream Symbols Dictionary

something is wrong.

Stars: children; an important person; a great number of people; your descendants; angels; Jesus Christ; fallen angels; if a falling star it can mean satan or an apostate church.

Statue: an idol; something in your life that you are worshipping or holding in ungodly value.

Statue of Liberty: the USA; Holy Spirit's liberty; freedom in Christ.

Steak: spiritual food for the mature person.

Steering Wheel: directions for the road of life; control over a person's life; if the wheel is in the back seat it means someone wants control over another's life.

Steps: you are moving in either the right or wrong direction; if steps lead upwards it can mean promotion, growing in maturity or you are on a difficult journey; if moving downward it can mean demotion or a pathway to death.

Stillborn: a long-awaited dream or desire has been carried to term and then dies.

Sting: mental torment; demonic torment; see bees.

Stirring: being the cause of strife, mischief or trouble; stirring up people in the faith or to good works; stirring up the gifts within you.

Stock Market: trusting in money; gambling in life.

Stomach: things of the flesh; not able to stomach something unpleasant in your life.

Stone: Jesus Christ as the chief cornerstone; a hard and sturdy foundation; the Word of God.

Stoning: someone involved in malicious accusation of others; un-forgiveness; wicked actions or motives; hardness of heart.

Stone faced: hardened and unrepentant of sin.

Stone Wall: an obstacle in your life or ministry; a person is being unmovable that can be either good or bad; a person is stone-walling; if the wall is broken it means there is a need to rebuild something in your life.

Stop Sign: telling you to stop a behavior or activity.

Storm: a trial or testing period; satanic attacks; distresses in life.

White Storm: God's power; revival.

Storm Clouds: being white or black will determine if either something good or bad is coming your way.

Stove: projects in one's life; something on the back burner; see oven.

Stopwatch: being under time constraints or pressure to perform; you are running out of time for a decision or opportunity.

Store: a variety of choices in life.

Storehouse: things stored up but only accessible only through God.

Straight: someone's attitude needs to be straightened up; no ambiguity in you or your situation; you are going in the right direction in life or a situation.

Straight Path: ease in life; being led by God.

Straining: under duress in a situation or with a relationship.

Straitjacket: mental, emotional or spiritual imprisonment; the enemy keeping you from your purpose or ministry.

Strangers: demons or angels depending on the context.

A to Z Christian Dream Symbols Dictionary

Strangulation: a spirit or someone trying to choke out one's faith or action; strangling yourself can mean an unsuccessful attempt to take control or move into position of power; if you are strangling someone else it means hatred for the person; if you are being strangled it is a warning about a physical, emotional or spiritual attack on you.

Straw: worthless words or valueless work; works that will be burned up one day.

Stream: life with Jesus; a stream that is deep when stepped into means life flowing from God.

Street: a public area in life; can be hypocrisy; evangelism.

Street Names: study all street name meanings and relevance to you.

Street Sign: God pointing you in the right direction in your life; God giving you a warning or a command.

Stretcher: injury or sickness; being carried by God in a time of spiritual weakness.

Strongman: a strong demonic spirit requiring spiritual warfare.

Stumbling: making mistakes or poor life decisions; stumbling in faith; failing in a task, ministry or relationship; being in error; a lack of the truth.

Student: a time of learning and submission in your life; if dreaming of being around students it can mean a position of authority over others; see school.

Studying: a wearisome activity.

Stump: a Godly remnant.

Stylus: entrenched habits.

Submarine: submission to authority; coming under a silent and hidden sneak attack; someone trying to torpedo you, a relationship or your ministry.

Suffocate: can be a sleep disorder; demonic activity; someone or something trying to suffocate you emotionally or spiritually; someone trying to suffocate your calling or ministry.

Sugar: sweetness of life; too much sugar can mean an imbalanced spiritual diet; you are telling people what they want to hear as opposed to what they need to hear; you or someone is sugar coating words.

Suicide: you are doing something that is bringing self-destruction; ruining one's own reputation; sinful behavior; pride; destiny; living by foolishness words, choices and actions; a lack of hope or depression.

Suing: unrighteous behavior.

Suit: you are serious and highly conscientious about what you want to do; you are dressed and prepared for spiritual battle or ministry.

Suitcase/Bag: baggage from one's past; a time of transition; you are prepared to move on in life; a call to missions or evangelism.

Sulfur: God's judgment against the wicked; something doesn't go down right with you.

Summer: a time of preparation; an opportune time; fruits of the Spirit; a time of making plans and working hard.

Summer Fruits: gladness and joy.

Sun: a reference to someone's father; a bright shining sun means God's goodness; fullness of life; the Son of God; the light of God; the truth; the glory of God; a darkened sun indicates a major disaster or destruction; can also mean endurance.

Sun, Moon and Stars: symbolic of order; can mean false worship or the occult.

A to Z Christian Dream Symbols Dictionary

Sunburn: a hard worker; you are affected by a great time spent with the Son of God.

Sunglasses: someone is trying to mask their true feelings, thoughts or intentions.

Sunrise: beginning of new thing, life or season; relief after a time or struggle and testing in life.

Sunset: the end of a thing, life or a season or good or bad; peace; tranquility; praising God.

Superheroes: supernatural abilities for spiritual warfare; being a superhero indicates your role in fighting injustice or forces of spiritual wickedness.

Supper: the body and blood of Jesus; the marriage supper; God's provision; God's enabling power.

Surfboard: riding a coming wave of success.

Surgery: the Great Physician repairing emotions or removing unwanted things and sin with His skilled hand.

Surgical Instruments: showing what or who God is using to remove things from your life.

Surrounded: being hated, slandered or attacked by others; being surrounded by God's love and protection in a time of great need or testing.

Swallowing: a symbol of blessing, peace or finding your place in life; not taking offense at other's words; swallowing your pride; refusing to retaliate or use hateful words.

Swarms: people or demonic spirits out to devour or destroy.

Swashbuckler: a person who is difficult to live with and who likes to argue.

Swearing/Cussing: an unclean spirit.

167

John Mark Volkots

Sweating: signs of intense work of the flesh; much work without Holy Spirit; a difficult and agonizing time.

Sweeping: getting rid of sinful things in your life; spiritually cleaning a place from evil through intercession; correcting a situation; repentance.

Sweets: something gratifying; reflecting on the Word of God; communion with Holy Spirit; negatively it can be a spirit of seduction; can mean gossip.

Swift: order and fast obedience to God's commands and desires.

Swimming: a time of leisure and rest; moving in the Spirit; prophetic utterance; trying to stay afloat; if you are being chased it can mean a spiritual or human enemy in your life; if you are with friends and family enjoying yourself it can mean fun and relaxation in life; if you are naked or topless while swimming it means a feeling of having your weaknesses exposed to other people.

Swimming Pool: a gathering place; a church; a place or provision available for moving in the Spirit; if the pool is dirty it can mean corrupt, apostate or evil activity around you; a clear pool means refreshing in or being immersed in Holy Spirit.

Swing: moving in the ups and downs of life.

Swinging: full flow of power; full flow of peace.

Swinging High: reaching for the high things of God; Flowing high in Holy Spirit; negatively it can mean overindulgence; taking unnecessary risks.

Sword: the Word of God; responding with the Word of God; the sword of God; a spiritual battle is going to be taking place; you are trying to defend yourself instead of letting God defend you; harsh or evil words.

Symphony: working in perfect union with others; it also indi-

A to Z Christian Dream Symbols Dictionary

cates prophesying; giving thanks to God.

T

Table: a place of agreement or covenant; a place of shared beliefs or interests; a place to iron out issues; an altar; a community; family; fellowship; if the table is dark it indicates ungodly activities in your life.

Tablet: your heart; your heart is ready to be inscribed upon.

Tabloid: having morbid interests in gossip or slander.

Tail: immature behavior; the end or least of something; being or feeling last or unimportant; feeling you or another is just tagging along; the last time; having a tail can also mean a false teacher; gossip or slander.

Tailor: an angel or Holy Spirit preparing you for a life event.

Talking Back: foolishness; rebellion.

Tall: feeling important in your own eyes or in the eyes of others; a person of high social standing; a person who feels they are above others or above the law.

Tambourine: celebration; joy; praise; worship.

Tank (Army): heavy protection; a militant attitude if heading towards others; if coming towards you it indicates a major assault coming against you either in the natural or spiritual realm.

Tanned: trying to make yourself look good either physically or spiritually.

A to Z Christian Dream Symbols Dictionary

Tape Measure: examining yourself or others to see if you or they measure up.

Tapeworm: can be anxieties about not being able to gain weight; feeling all your efforts are failing or being eaten up.

Tar: feeling trapped or stuck in a situation; a covering; bitterness.

Tarantula: a sorcerer; a demonic spirit.

Tares: children of darkness; evil or deceptive people; degenerate people.

Target: aiming for a goal; targeting someone or something which can be good or bad; if you are wearing the target you are the target of a person or a demon.

Tarot Cards: demonic; fortune telling.

Tasting: to experience something either good or bad; trying something out; testing the waters in a circumstance; judging.

Taskmaster: a harsh or overbearing person in a position of authority.

Tattoo: worldliness; pagan rituals; occult or occult influence; rebellion.

Tea/Iced Tea: a place or time of refreshing; a revelation of God's grace.

Teacher: a pastor; a teacher; Jesus; Holy Spirit; a gift from God; an authority figure.

Tears: emotional sowing which is usually distress, but could also represent brokenness; hurt; sorrow; a broken heart; repentance; a longing for God; tears of joy.

Teenager/s: carelessness; a youthful life; exuberance.

Teeth/Chewing. Wisdom; gaining understanding; ability to

171

comprehend or understand a situation; need for understanding; need for a mature spiritual diet; need to work something out; symbolic of a person's words; someone who likes to tell fanciful stories.

Baby Teeth: childish; without wisdom or knowledge; inexperienced.

Broken Teeth: can be anguish; mourning and bitterness in life; difficulty in coming to understanding.

Brushing Teeth: gaining wisdom or understanding.

Clean Teeth: not having any food physically or spiritually; a spiritual drought.

Cracked Teeth: fear of dying or aging.

False Teeth: full of worldly reasoning instead of pure spiritual understanding.

Missing Teeth: feeling like not having anything to say; not allowed to have any say in a matter.

Seeing Teeth Shatter: God is fighting against your enemies; if it is your teeth it means God is fighting against something you are doing.

Losing or Teeth Falling Out: losing ability to think things through; losing ability to consume a healthy spiritual diet; fear of getting old; feeling your life is decaying; can mean a fast lifestyle.
Incisor Teeth: an ability to make good decisions.

Losing Eye Teeth: losing ability to understand prophetic things.

Losing Wisdom Teeth: an inability to make proper or wise decisions.

A to Z Christian Dream Symbols Dictionary

Sharp or Razor Teeth: using words like weapons against people or the enemy.

Toothache: tribulation or heartache coming; someone or something is a source of constant irritation or pain.

Telephone: spiritual communication that can be good or bad; communication with others but mainly with God; Godly counsel.

Telescopes: a prophetic gift; looking or planning for the future; making a problem bigger and closer than it really is.

Television: visionary revelation; prophetic dreams or prophetic utterance; media arts; idleness; being unproductive; you are allowing distractions in your life.

Temple: a place of meeting with God; a place of refuge and safety; God's habitation; your body; negatively a pagan temple or pagan influence.

Tennis: being in competition with someone; the one who begins the game is the one who is serving or instigating the competition; can be friendly or adverse competition.

Tent: a temporary covering; a temporary living situation; long term or frequent travel; being flexible; our body; an elaborate or colorful tent can mean the secret place of God.

Termites: small spiritual attacks eating away at you or eating away at your faith's foundation; tiny things that upset you that you can't seem to fix or get rid of.

Terror: fear of death; fear of a major attack; a demonic spirit of terror.

Test: being tested by life's trials; a lesson to learn.

Text Messages: receiving prophetic words; receiving directions or commands from God.

173

Theatre: living on the stage of life with others watching; being in a theater with dead people indicates you have wandered away from the truth.

Thermometer/Fever: spiritual infection in you or the Church Body.

Thief: satan or demons sent to kill, steal and destroy your peace, joy, love, dreams, destiny or your life; a deceiver; a secret intruder; an unexpected loss.

Thigh: a covenant or oath taken; strength; faith; flesh; enticement or seduction.

Thirst: spiritual thirst for Jesus the Living Water; thirsting after God; feeling in a dry place in your life; longing for something in life either good or bad.

Three Sets of Double Doors: you need to make a choice on three issues; three choices to make about one issue or situation.

Thorns: sin; worries; trials; life's cares choking your faith; Christ's suffering for your sins.

Thread: something in your life is hanging by a thread; a non-believer who has decided to place their trust in Jesus.

Throne: a seat of power; a place of authority; God's throne; authority or sovereignty over a place or situation; an evil throne; satan's place of power or authority.

Throwing: throwing someone indicates banishment.

Throw up Dreams: same as going to the bathroom; God is cleaning you of toxins in your life.

Thumb: apostolic; authority; soul power.

Thumbs-up: approval; authorized for an assignment.

A to Z Christian Dream Symbols Dictionary

Thunder: a loud signal from God to you or others; a warning; blessings, God's anger; a loud voice in your life.

Tick: something or someone draining you and infecting you emotionally or spiritually.

Ticket: a coming journey or entrance into a new place in life; an invitation to spend time with God; being written a ticket by a police officer is a Godly warning before you suffer consequences for your action or behavior.

Tidal Wave: an overwhelming conflict or attack; an overwhelming disaster; see hurricane; floods.

Tie: a neat and professional appearance; trying to be presentable to God or others.

Tiger: may represent a sudden surprise attack in the natural or spiritual realm; a person or spiritual enemy attempting to stalk and devour.

Tightrope: having to watch one's steps to avoid danger or a spiritual fall; trying to keep your emotions together in a difficult time or situation; trying to keep relationships together during a difficult time or situation; trying to keep balance in a life that is too busy.

Tight Space: a situation in life that is suffocating or difficult.

Tin: something of low value; not original; an imitation; worthless dross or toxins in your life.

Tires: your ability to move in life; where the rubber meets the road; gaining traction in life or in ministry.

Flat Tire: shows inconvenience; inability to go anywhere or make progress.

Bald Tire: may mean an inability to get a grip on what God has called you to do,

Good Tires: you have traction in life to get where you are going.

Aired up Tires: Holy Spirit is going to ride and power you there.

Titanic: big plan or desire will not work out.

Title/Deed: seal of ownership; an idea or project; a potential to possess something in the physical or spiritual realm.

Toad: demonic spirits.

Tobacco: indicates bad habits or addictions.

Toilet: you are in a vulnerable and susceptible position; exposure; a need to flush something out of your life; being flushed down a toilet means you are flushing your life away or flushing away the hard and dirty path to a new place.

Toll Booth: you are going to have to pay the cost to go higher in God; you are going to pay the cost of ungodly living or ungodly choices in life.

Tomb: death; a hypocrite.

Tombstone: death; death to a dream, ministry or position; the inscription on the stone will give more insight.

Tongue: a call to use your spiritual language; your words are deciding your future; what you are speaking is giving power to either life or death of something; there is something in your life that you cannot get control of or over; a split or cut tongue indicates confusion and perversion.

Tooth: see teeth.

Toothache: see teeth.

A to Z Christian Dream Symbols Dictionary

Toothpaste: a need to clean up one's mouth, speech or attitude; a need to stop cursing or complaining.

Topaz: someone or something highly valuable in life.

Topless: exposure in life; if you did not feel ashamed it means you are comfortable about yourself in public; you are being open and vulnerable.

Tornado: a distressing situation; great danger; a warning of a coming danger or attack; spiritual warfare; a call to pray; if white means it is from God and dark from the enemy; multiple tornadoes indicates multiple problems in your life at the same time.

Tourist: being in a temporary place in life; you are looking at something or a situation from the outside; a feeling you don't belong to a group or situation.

Tow Truck: helping other people out of problems in life.

Towel: being of service or a servant to others; humility.

Tower: a place of refuge; a high spiritual thing; a supernatural experience; great strength; pride as in the tower of Babel.

Toy: something regarded as unnecessary; something desired for amusement or gratification.

Track: the race of life you are in; a coming challenge.

Tractor (Farm): ground breaking ministry; preparing the mind to receive; potential harvest; greater & faster return for your spiritual sowing,

Traffic: not being able to go where you want in life as fast as you want.

Traffic Light: life direction; see road signs.

Red: need to stop doing something or going somewhere.

177

Yellow: a need to proceed with caution in a situation or with a person.

Green: permission to go forward with a ministry or something in your life.

Trailer: an equipping ministry; a caring service; a ministry that is migrating.

Train: a large ministry that influences many people; a fast moving ministry; a ministry to send people out.

Train Track: fixed or on track to your destination which can be good or bad.

Trampled: feeling trampled indicates oppression by a natural or spiritual enemy.

Trampoline: enjoying life; lots of up and down activity in your spiritual life but not able to get anywhere or maintain any true lasting progress.

Translator: helping others understand or interpreting things for others.

Trap: evil scheme against you by others or the demonic realm; can mean a coming and hidden snare in life; a feeling you are trapped in life

Trapper: a deadly enemy; someone trying to catch you in your words for no good.

Trash: something worthless and without value in your life; trash on someone's face indicates rebuke from God.

Treasure: God's Word; your value to God and others.

Treasure Chest: finding great spiritual truth that had been hidden from you; hidden prizes, awards and spiritual jewels.

A to Z Christian Dream Symbols Dictionary

Tree/Trees: people; leaders either good or bad; a church or organization; nations or kingdoms.

Green Tree: a prosperous person.

Uprooted Tree: a false teacher or prophet; someone who is spiritually dead.

Christmas Tree: celebrations; salvation is coming to deliver you from sin, others or a situation.

Evergreen Tree: a long-lasting relationship or situation.

Oak Tree: great strength; durable; God's people.

Olive Tree: anointed of God; Israel; the Church; anointing oil.

Palm Tree: a leader who is producing fruit; one who stands tall in any situation.

Tree Stump: tenacity or stubbornness; always retaining hope despite circumstances; keeping your roots in place.

Willow Tree: indicating sadness; defeat; weakness.

Tree of Life: indicates wisdom; making correct choices in life; feeding off of Jesus.

Tricycle: childishness; a beginning ministry.

Triplets: coming triple blessing or a triple alliance of friends.

Triple Braided Rope: strength; unity.

Tripping: to be tripped or to trip someone is an attempt to cause failure in one's life.

Trojan Horse: disguised anger; a disguised attack.

Troops: war; being under siege.

Trophy: victory; coming award or reward; God's recognition; promotion from others or God.

Truck: rough lifestyle for a non-believer; personal ministry that brings provision; large ministry; corporate move of God; size of truck determines the size of ministry or move of God.

Trumpet: the voice of the prophet; the second coming of Jesus; celebration or praise; proclaiming the good news; blessings; a promise; a call to war.

Tsunami: a stressful event; tribulation; sudden destruction; feeling overwhelmed or about to be overwhelmed by people or a situation.

Tug-of-War: friendly completion between friends; competition with a call to pray for peace with the person shown.

Tulips: speech & your two lips, see mouth, tongue.

Tumbleweed: wicked person's life; destruction; blown about in life.

Tumor: something in your life that is causing pain and/or spiritual death that needs to be dealt with; may be a call to prayer.

Tunnel: a passage through a mountain in your life; a time or place of transition; troubled or dark seasons of life; someone or something taking you somewhere with little direction or light.

Turban: righteousness; justice.

Turkey (Bird): either wisdom or foolishness; foolish people; a number of turkeys could mean a number of circumstances that could bring embarrassment.

Turtle: can mean peace; slowness in action; withdrawn; a spirit of stupor; a cautious person; being or feeling protected; feeling safe; steady.

Turtledove: affectionate; gentle; love; shy.

A to Z Christian Dream Symbols Dictionary

Tuxedo: formality.

Twins: double-portion anointing or blessing on your life.

Two Cents: a worthless opinion; small acts of obedience seen by God.

Two Parallel Gold Ribbons: two things God wants to accomplish through the one wearing the ribbon.

Two People Doing Something to Each Other Who Are The Same People: you are doing something very destructive to yourself.

Two People Having Same Dream: strong confirmation to what you are doing or about to do.

Two Story: multi-level gifted person; multi gifted ministry or church; symbolic of flesh and spirit.

U-V

UFO: indicates heavenly visitors either demons or angels.

Umbilical Cord: being attached to someone or something which can be good or bad depending on the context; your connection to life and spiritual nourishment; can indicate a need to detach from someone or something to have your own life as an individual.

Umbrella: God's protection; personal covering or protection in life's storms; if it is raining and you have no umbrella it means you are unprepared or unprotected from life's storms.

Umpire: an advocate; Jesus; someone who is refereeing between people; Holy Spirit; a leader or good friend.

Underwater Dreams: deep things of the Spirit.

Unicycle: moving through life awkwardly or attempting to keep your balance in a tricky situation.

Uniform: conformity or unity; belonging to a certain group.

Universe: God's eternal creativity.

University: advanced spiritual authority; high level spiritual warfare equipping; advanced spiritual growth.

Upstairs: deep or things of Holy Spirit; the spiritual realm where we do spiritual warfare; great balance in life.

Upward Motion: moving into higher spiritual matters or growth.

A to Z Christian Dream Symbols Dictionary

Urinating: releasing the pressure of life; having a compelling temptation or urge; repentance; urinating in someone's house means you feel you have lost control of your emotions or embarrassed yourself in front of others; to see someone urinating in your house can mean you perceive that person has committed an offensive act against you.

Usher: can stand for tradition; serving others.

Vacation: emotional or spiritual refreshment and rest.

Vacuum: if in use it shows a need to remove dirt from the object or person shown.

Vagrant: an outcast; a wanderer; an emotional or spiritual murderer.

Valedictorian: being praised for doing well.

Valentine: romance; love; your relationship with Jesus.

Valley: a low point in your life; territory of an enemy.

Vampires: a demon or someone who sucks the life out of you; a bad or evil influence.

Van/Moving Van: see automobiles.

Vapor: our natural life; fleeting wealth; a temporary situation or circumstance; the presence of God; evidence of something.

Vault: see safe.

Vegetables: a healthy spiritual diet; eating vegetables may imply meekness or humble circumstances.

Vehicles: bicycles, cars, scooters, usually speak of size or level of gifting, ministry or work that you are doing; can also refer to a secular job; for non-believers it can mean the ride of life or lifestyle; also see automobiles.

Buses: typically represent churches or larger areas of impact to many people.

Trains: usually means a large church, denomination, ministry or corporation.

Small Airplanes: about the same as a car or bike; think about size and occupancy levels such as row boats verses larger boats.

Sail Boat: represents freedom in life or ministry because it uses the wind of Holy Spirit; always look at what you are doing on a boat, plane or other vehicles; the captain on a large ship would refer to a pastor or boss.

Veil: to hide glory or sin; to deceive someone; being blind to the truth; a lack of understanding.

Vein: contains the blood or spiritual life condition of a person.

Venom: destructive language or activities; someone with venomous mouth and words.

Ventriloquist: someone not in control of their life; being controlled by others or the demonic realm.

Vertigo: out of balance or off-balance in your life.

Vessel: people as instruments for good or bad purposes; believers; a container of treasure or blessings; a container of anointing.

Vest: a need for protection.

Veteran: one who has been trained and has vast experience in spiritual warfare.

Veterinarian: having compassion; helping those with no voices to be heard; helping the helpless.

Vice Grips: under strong pressure; stress; held in a position or situation against your will; holding onto something very tightly.

A to Z Christian Dream Symbols Dictionary

Victory: being victorious in a battle means having wise counsel in life.

Video Game: being in a video game can symbolize your life; feeling life is a game; it can also mean you are spending too much time on useless activity.

Village: a community or group of people close to you; group seclusion.

Viking: a strong or fierce fighter in the spiritual realm.

Vine: Jesus; believers; an outstretched vine can mean great influence.

Vinegar: reproaches and slandering by a human or demonic enemy; a person with a sour or biting disposition.

Vineyard: harvest; a place of planting; a heavenly kingdom; God's vineyard; God's people; if the vineyard is overgrown with thorns and weeds it indicates laziness.

Violin: soothing and pleasant activities; romance; God serenading you.

Violence: being shot, stabbed, raped or murdered means demonic attacks.

Viper: see snakes.

Virgin: a believer; the church; an actual virgin.

Virgin Mary: the Lord's favor; to dream of Mary blocking your view of Jesus may indicate a need to refocus your worship on Jesus.

Vitamins: doing things that are good for you or needing to do things that are good for you; you may need to supplement your spiritual diet through things such as teaching and preaching.

Voices: restlessness; distractions; pressure from the enemy; demonic voices; a message from God or satan; the Word of God; Godly instruction; worldly temptations.

Volcano: an unpredictable, unstable and out of control person; judgment; a sudden and explosive person or circumstance.

Vomit: rolling in vomit indicates being humiliated.

Vomiting: getting rid of something unwanted in your life; being mentally, physically or spiritually poisoned by an environment or ungodly influence; eating vomit indicates repeating bad behavior.

Voodoo Doll: a need to pray against witchcraft and curses being spoken over you.

Vultures: a vulgar or wicked person; being unclean or impure; being ravaged by the demonic realm; a human or spiritual enemy out to devour or pick you apart.

W

Wading: experimenting or testing the waters in a situation; afraid to go deeper in the Lord.

Wagons: a trailblazing or pioneering spirit; you are carrying burdensome things or other's burdens.

Waiter: serving others; someone who serves spiritual food; a deacon.

Waking: a need for spiritual awakening.

Walking: peace; tranquility; contentment in life; walking in the path of life; living in the Spirit, slow but continual spiritual progress.

Difficulty Walking: a trial or evil opposition to your destiny.

Unable to Walk: a hindrance to doing what you were called to do; someone or something hindering you.

Walking With Another: complete agreement and unity.

Wall: an obstacle or barrier to your destiny, calling or ministry; a defense mechanism to keep people at a distance; a great hindrance; something blocking you from spiritual signs; hiding behind a wall means seeking protection; a leaning wall means you are under pressure; a flimsy wall can mean folly of trusting in wealth; a broken wall means not having self-control.

Wallet: wealth or finances.

War: spiritual warfare; a call to prayer.

Warehouse: a storehouse of God's provision for you.

Warlock: people influenced by demonic religious practices have been recruited to influence people or a situation; see psychics, witches.

Washing: represents holiness or cleansing from sin.

Wash Basin: a means of cleansing; prayer and intercession.

Wash Cloth: receiving help in getting dirt or sin out of your life or helping others get dirt or sin out of their life.

Washing Machine: a deep cleansing in your life.

Wasps: someone with a biting tongue; spirits of terror and confusion; see bees.

Watch/Clock: a need to be watchful; watching for something to happen; time for something to occur; a call to be a watchman on the wall; God's timing for you individually.

Watchdog: God's guardianship for you or the person in the dream; a call for you to be a watchman and stand in the gap for someone.

Watchmen: a prophet; an intercessor

Water: Holy Spirit; a move of Holy Spirit; nations of the world; Jesus is the water of life; can also stand for humanity; precedes birth of a dream, vision or ministry; brings cleansing; implies baptism.

Water in a Cloud: depends on whether the cloud is white or grey that will determine if something good or bad is coming.

Stagnant/Muddy/Polluted: corrupted spiritual moves; sin; false doctrine.

Troubled Water: a healing pool of ministry; a troubled mind.

Water Fountain: God's Spirit welling up within man; good words; life; salvation.

Water Well: revival coming; a time of refreshing; a place of spiritual food; a person's heart.

Waterfall: a place of peace and rest during life's journey; overwhelming refreshment after a long climb in life; if the waterfall is raging it can mean a long difficult climb or descent in your progress in life.

Water Tower: a man-made water tower means trusting in something other than God.

Watering: generous giving; a person who builds others up.

Watermelon: fruitfulness; sweetness; a Spirit ruled life.

Waves: tumultuous people or a stormy time in life; carried by the Spirit or a move of Holy Spirit; swept up in blessings and love; grief; danger; can also mean false doctrine; trickery and deceit.

Wax: a faint heart over a situation.

Wedding: new beginnings; joy; happiness.

Wedding Cake: matrimony; unending love.

Weeds: a sinful nature; sinful actions; evil and wicked people; unbelievers.

Weight: great load or burden; great responsibility.

Werewolf: people whose actions and attitudes can turn them into a monster; a spiritual enemy.

West: see directions.

Whale: running from God; being devoured by a large problem or situation.

Wheat: a believer; legitimacy; God's Word.

Wheel: your life as a whole; something long lasting; something continuous which can be bad or good depending on the context; someone or something going to move you to action.

Wheelchair: being carried in life; recovering from emotional hurts; needing help in life.

Whip: a curse; stubbornness.

Whirlwind: calamity; if you survive the wind it signifies your righteousness; a powerful move in the Spirit.

Whispering: hateful words; gossip or slander; enemies taking counsel against you.

Whistle: calling someone; a time out; a warning.

White Monsters and White Witches: someone or something appearing to be righteous and holy but are actually destructive and deadly.

Wife: actual wife; person joined to you in covenant; spirit of submission; the Church; Israel.

Wilderness: feeling spiritual dryness; hard times in life; a place of trial & testing; feeling distant from God; place of training; place of provision.

Willow Tree: weeping; mourning; sorrow; fragile in the storms of life.

Wind: move of the Spirit which can be good or evil; stormy wind means troubles; something or someone disappears quickly from your life; unstable person; person hard to understand.

Window: a person's eyes; prophetic gifting; revelation knowledge; gaining insight.

Wine: Holy Spirit; Christ's blood; communion; teaching; blessing; a counterfeit spirit.

A to Z Christian Dream Symbols Dictionary

Wine Press: feeling your emotional or spiritual life is being squeezed out of you; true doctrine.

Wineskins: the body or church of Christ.

Winged Women: a class of angelic beings.

Wing/Wings: freedom; rest from troubles; a swift movement or change of position; the prophetic; being under God's protection; a period not suitable for work; someone who lifts you to higher places in God.

Wink: approval; acknowledgement; deception; someone not serious; allurement of seduction.

Winter: peace; tranquility; season of unfruitfulness; latent period; late time in a person's life.

Wisdom: riches; honor; peace; long life.

Wisdom Teeth: see teeth.

Witch: you or someone in your life is involved in witchcraft; a spirit of rebellion; someone who is non- submissive; a manipulative and controlling person; a spirit of control.

Wizard: see psychics.

Wolf/Wolves: people out to destroy you or destroy God's work; a false minister; a demonic attack; a demonic attack through people; an opportunistic person; a vicious person.

Woman: a helper; a loud woman means unwise living; a woman in dark clothing means a spiritual enemy; a woman clothed in purple means a good wife.

Woman (Unknown): angel; demonic spirit; a seducing spirit.

Wood: life; humanity; carnal reasoning; lust; depending on flesh; can also be compassion because it is not hard or cold like metal.

Woods: feeling lost in life; feeling alone or isolated from people or God.

Wooden Raft: Godly things you have built in your life that can bring you safely through life's storms, but you may have left gaps in your life that may need to be filled.

Wool: pure living; angel hair.

Working: profit; a provider; context or what you are working at will give more answers.

Workshop/Work Area: a place or area of ministry; God's process of building your life.

Worm: disgrace; contempt; repugnance; something that is eating you from the inside often secretly; something not obvious on the surface but still damaging to your emotional or spiritual life; disease; filthiness; humility.

Wormwood: bitterness in life; feeling bitter towards yourself or others.

Wound: an unhealed emotional hurt; a wounded relationship calling for healing; unconfessed sin.

Wreath: may be a holiday timeline clue; if on the head it symbolizes wisdom; symbol of teaching & instruction from wise parents.

Wrestler: a human or spiritual enemy.

Wrestling: battling another person, God or the devil; if wrestling with a stranger it means struggling against an evil spirit; may be telling you to contend with perseverance; are struggling in your emotional, spiritual or actual life.

Wristwatch: if you keep checking your watch it indicates anxiety over an issue.

Writing: expressing something you never got a chance to say to a friend or relative; pay attention to what was written and who it was written to.

X-Y-Z

X: an area of significance or particular interest; can indicate hidden earthly or spiritual treasures.

Xerox (Copy Machine): repetition or endless cycles of a situation; copying someone's behavior, speech or attitude.

X-ray: having intense perception and spiritual discernment about the true intentions of a person; high spiritual discernment about a situation.

Yard: your home life; the open part of who you are that you allow others to see; your personality; the back yard can also mean what is in your life that is out of sight, below the surface or in the past.

Yarn: good deeds towards others.

Yawning: boredom; fatigue.

Year: a time of blessing or judgment.

Yearbook: reviewing your life's actions which can be good or bad.

Yeast: cause others to rise up in gifts & calling; religious behaviors that puff you up; hypocrisy.

Yelling: irritating or annoying situations or people; feeling you cannot be heard; someone attempting to disrupt peace, others or a situation.

A to Z Christian Dream Symbols Dictionary

Yield: a need or call to submission; also see road signs.

Yin-Yang: someone influenced by ungodly Asian philosophy.

Yoga: influences of Hinduism; Buddhism; Jainism or Sikhism.

Yogurt: trying to live healthy emotionally and spiritually.

Yoke: slavery or in bondage to something or someone; you are tied to something usually evil but sometimes good; Christ's mastery over your life; also can be a need to submit to authority.

Young Girl: a young church or ministry; an actual young girl.

Yo-Yo: indecisiveness; up and down in your spiritual or emotional life.

You Are a Child: there are some issues in your life God wants to deal with and release you from so you can grow; your soul got stunted and you stopped developing and God wants you to grow; satan stopped you from growing but God is working to grow you up.

Zealot: intense fervor and drive for God and His kingdom; intense fervor and drive for a cause which can be good or bad.

Zebra: a black or white situation that calls for an unequivocal decision; something that is clearly right or wrong in your life.

Zeppelin: impending disaster; a call to pray over an impending disaster.

Zero: something with no value; a feeling you have no value.

Ziggurat: pagan worship; idolatry; man's arrogance.

Zinc: feeling a need for or needing protection.

Zion: a place of strength and protection; leadership; God's kingdom.

John Mark Volkots

Zipper/Button on Lips: a sign that you are to keep quiet about or in a situation.

Zodiac Signs/Horoscopes: magic and sorcery to be avoided; mythology; false predicting of the future.

Zombies: spiritually lost people who are dead in sin.

Zoo: a busy and active place in life.

NUMBERS

One: the number of God; unity that can't be divided; beginning of the first; eternal wholeness; independence; can also mean attached as it excludes all things that are different.

Two: blessing; double portion; agreement; covenant; unity; believers ministry; witnessing; confirmation; wholeness in marriage; separation or division; judgment; multiplication; discord and war.

Three/Third: witness; divine fullness; resurrection; conforming; triumph over sin; triumph over the enemy; restoration; balance; perfect testimony, obedience; invincibility; divine completeness and perfection; confirmation or approval; the Godhead or Trinity; things that have become solid and complete; associated with spirit and life.

Four: God's creative intelligence; God's creative works; God's creative works in redemption; reigning; dominion; the heavens; angels; the vastness of space, global implication of the gospel; worldly creations; the four corners of the world; four mind; four seasons,

Five: God's grace; atonement; redemption; the goodness of God; blessings; a new song; anointing; fruitfulness; a life that's moved by Holy Spirit; freedom and completeness; grace related to the five-fold ministry.

Six: harmony; cooperation; marriage; beauty, the number of humanity; weakness of the flesh; human labor or human completeness; can also describe the battle between our spirit and flesh.

666: the number of satan; the counterfeit of God's Trinity; the mark of the beast; humanity.

Seven: perfection; completion; purification; consecration; sovereignty; the covenant between man and God.

Eight: the new birth; new beginnings; infinity; resurrection; strength; circumcision of the flesh; fertility; someone who abounds in physical, emotional or spiritual strength.

888: major restoration; major new beginnings.

Nine: describes the perfect movement of God; Holy Spirit; an evangelist; fullness of blessings; fruit of the Spirit; gift of the Spirit; harvest or fruit of your labor; salvation; judgment or finality of things; judgment of Man and his works; can also mean ingratitude.

Ten: trial or testing; law; order; government; governmental order and obligation; earthly or heavenly law; responsibility; completeness that happens in a divine order or during a course of time; the tithe or God's portion; the number of pastoral; compassion; journey; wilderness.

Eleven: number of the prophetic, a prophetic anointing; revelation; transition; a paradigm shift; the end or finish; confusion; things of imperfection; disorganization of systems; disorder or chaos of things; lawlessness; judgment.

Twelve: number of the apostolic; divine government and order; divine perfect order and power; New Jerusalem.

Thirteen: the number of rebellion or spiritual depravity; backsliding; corruption; abandonment; defection; revolution; to break or destroy; superstition

Fourteen: deliverance or salvation; double anointing; recreation; reproduction; Passover; spiritual perfection that is doubled

Fifteen: mercy; grace; liberty; freedom; pardon; a reprieve; rest; energy that's found within acts of divine Grace.

Sixteen: love; being set free by love; the power of love or salvation; established beginnings; to have passion; to cherish and have devotion towards someone or something.

Seventeen: victory; election or the elect; perfection of spiritual order; spiritual process of maturity; not yet matured.

Eighteen: established blessings; established judgment; things that deal with bondage, slavery, or captivity; blessing or judgment of a ministry; a valiant person.

Nineteen: faith; repentance; perfection of divine order in judgment.

Twenty: attainment; a crowning accomplishment; holiness and redemption; fit for battle; expecting things to happen of a great magnitude.

Twenty One: divine completion of things.

Twenty Two: disorganization of things to a great degree; magnification of corruption and disintegration.

Twenty Three: things or situations that involve death or extinction.

Twenty Four: the elders in heaven; church elders; elderly wisdom; heavenly government; heavenly worship; completed order of God.

Twenty-five: beginning of pastoral or ministry training; expectancy of receiving divine grace and redemption from almighty God.

Twenty Six: reference with the Gospel of Jesus Christ.

Twenty Seven: expectancy of divine approval or redemption.

Twenty Eight: expectancy of divine strength and courage.

Twenty Nine: expectancy of judgment.

Thirty: beginning of ministry or ministry training ; maturity for God's work; ministry maturity; the price of redemption; the blood of Jesus; dedication; a marking of the right moment.

Thirty One: things that deal with the names of God or Deity.

Thirty Two: a covenant or agreement with someone or a group.

Thirty Three: making a pledge or promise to someone.

Thirty Four: the naming of a son.

Thirty Five: hope, trust or confidence in a person or situation.

Thirty Six: a particular enemy or opposition.

Thirty Seven: a word that comes from God.

Thirty Eight: slavery; complete control over someone.

Thirty Nine: having a sickness or disease.

Forty: total rule; trial, probation; testing; divine judgment.

Forty Two: refers to the antichrist.

Forty Four: things that bring about a worldwide divine judgment against humanity.

Forty Five: maintaining, preserving or protecting things that matter the most to you.

Fifty: Pentecost; freedom; a time or year of jubilee; hope; humble service; number for Holy Spirit; deliverance; being set free from debt; restoration of things.

A to Z Christian Dream Symbols Dictionary

Fifty One: receiving divine revelation.

Sixty: an acceptable image; pride; arrogance; conceit.

Sixty Six: secular or idol worship; fallacy; trickery; guile and deception.

Seventy: God's administration; insight; restoration; impartation of God's Spirit; increase; negatively it can mean exile, punishment or captivity by an enemy.

Seventy-Five: a period for purification and separation.

Eighty: speech; beginning of a high calling; feeling spiritually acceptable; a strong and full life.

Ninety: the righteousness of God; being accepted; a devout person.

Ninety Nine: people and nations ripe and ready for harvest; a lost person; a prodigal.

One Hundred: God's election of grace; a full reward or return; the children of promise; the election process of God's chosen ones; completeness; abundance; fruitfulness; maturity.

One Hundred Eleven: my beloved one.

One Hundred and Nineteen: having success or mastery over something.

One Hundred-twenty: the end of flesh living and the beginning of life in the Spirit; the beginning of Holy Spirit's work in someone or something; the number or end of your days; a divine probation period.

One Hundred and Forty Four: having a personal human spiritual guide.

One Hundred Fifty: the promise; the Holy Spirit.

One Hundred Fifty Three: kingdom multiplication.

Two Hundred: fullness confirmed; a promise guaranteed; negatively it is things within a state of insufficiency.

Three Hundred: a faithful remnant; a valiant people; God's protection; the character of God; chosen by God; reserved of the Lord.

Four Hundred: truth; the Eternal King; fulfillment; Divinely perfect period in time.

Five Hundred: full service.

Six Hundred: extreme conflict or war.

Six Hundred and Sixty Six: humanity; the antichrist; the beast; satan; the end times.

Seven Hundred: completely full; choice warriors; accuracy in battle.

Seven Hundred and Seventy Seven: reference with the name of Jesus Christ.

Eight Hundred and Eighty Eight: reference with the Name of Holy Spirit.

Nine Hundred: full harvest.

One Thousand: the beginning of maturity; divine completeness; perfect fruitfulness; mature service; full status; millennial reign.

Eleven Hundred: silver.

Twelve Hundred: unity of the multitude.

Fifteen Hundred: authority; light; power.

Four Thousand: worldwide salvation.

A to Z Christian Dream Symbols Dictionary

Six Thousand: deception the antichrist will bring against humanity.

Seven Thousand: final judgment.

Ten Thousand: a big trial; the army of the Lord; ready for battle.

Eleven Thousand: the end of time.

Twelve Thousand: beautiful unity.

Twenty Thousand: a big decision.

Thirty Thousand: greatness and maturity in battle; strong in the Lord.

Forty Thousand: wise rule; skillful; expert.

Fifty Thousand: major trial by fire.

Sixty Thousand: the second advent.

Ninety Thousand: a very large harvest.

One Hundred Thousand: a great trial.

One Hundred and Forty Four Thousand: ones who come out of the great tribulation; the number for martyrs.

Thousands: approved maturity.

COLORS

Amber: contamination; idolatry; holiness or purity.

Black: black always stands for evil; always subtracts from life; stands for lack; famine; evil; demonic spirits; spiritual darkness; a person or figure in black is almost always an enemy; black skies and dark surroundings indicate your mood or the spiritual atmosphere of an area; although black or dark dreams come from the enemy, they can be good because what they are bringing can be defeated in prayer.

Blue: wisdom; holiness; grace; divine revelation; revelation about a matter is coming; a heaven related visitation from God or Holy Spirit; negatively it can mean emotional woes, anxiety and depression; a persons with dark blue eyes or dark blue skin can be demonic.

Light Blue: provision; rest and peace; good life; purity; conscience; envy; pride.

Brass or Bronze: judgment.

Brown/Tan: life; a change of season in life; born again; compassion; a pastoral color; man's natural qualities; earthly wisdom; humanism or manmade compassion.

Gold/Amber: wisdom; a seal of divinity; God's glory; God's mercy; faithfulness; endurance; purity; holiness that endures; a symbol of honor; of high valor; something valuable that endures; hallowed; holy; purity; negatively it can stand for greed or contamination.

Green: new life; prosperity; praise; provision; restoration; healing; rest; peace; a good life; negatively it stands for a seared conscience; envy and pride.

Grey: uncertainty; compromise; a mixture of good and bad; symbolic of death.

Orange: warning; danger ahead; caution needed; perseverance; stubbornness.

Orange or Yellow/Red: fire; Holy Spirit; earthly qualities; danger.

Pink: love; flesh or natural desires; not showing great passion for the things of God.

Plum: richness; abundance; infilling of Holy Spirit.

Purple: royalty; kingship; majesty; kingly anointing or authority.

Red: love; courage; heat or trials in life; passion; the blood of Jesus; the atonement; strong feelings about someone or something; wisdom; power; redemption; anointing; negatively it can mean danger; anger; war and destruction.

Silver: redemption; understanding; knowledge; an object or person of value; negatively it means worldly knowledge; betrayal; furnace of affliction.

White: purity; holiness; blamelessness; righteousness; innocence; the light and glory of God; white in the negative stands for things that appear to be righteous and holy, but in reality are deadly and destructive

Scarlet: the blood of Jesus; can also mean of sin in someone's life.

Yellow: something of high value; celebration; joy; hope; negatively it stands for cowardly, fear; the mind.

APPENDIX

Dream Interpretation Guidelines

The following guidelines are from notes taken while sitting under the teachings of John Paul Jackson, along with some additional guidelines of other dream interpreters.

Twenty categories of dreams

Body Dreams: Dreams that come from physical ailments, or chemical changes in your body due to everything from sickness, drugs (both prescription and illegal), or to extreme stress. Your body is making adjustments in fighting off these ailments and the dream depicts the warfare. They can also come from

A to Z Christian Dream Symbols Dictionary

chemical changes during pregnancies which can cause strange dreams. The baby can also dream and the mother can dream the babies dream, and they can co-mingle causing confusing dreams.

Calling dreams: Reveals the calling, ministry, or vocation God has created us for. It tells where we are going with it and how it is going to work in our life. It may also reveal details about our ministry and anointing He has for us or that are coming our way.

Chemical Dreams: Drugs of any kind whether legal or illegal, alcohol, pain relievers, and anything that alters our chemical make-up can have adverse effects on our dreams.

Comfort dreams: Lets you know God feels your heartache and wants you to know that He is there for you.

Correction Dreams: God may be telling us that we are going in the wrong direction or going about something the wrong way, so we can change our way. He helps us and encourages us to get back on the correct path. (Job 33:14)

Courage Dreams: In Genesis 31, God told Jacob that He wanted him to change the way his whole nation does business. He told him to take the stripped (mutant) and spotted or ugly cattle and he would make him a mighty nation. The normal procedure was to destroy any mutant cattle, but God gave him courage to go against what he was taught. God also used a dream of the enemy to give Gideon courage. (Judges 7:13-15)

Dark Dreams: Grey scale, muted color, black and white dreams, no or very little color or maybe one object that is a muted color. There is some or muted color but everything else is black and white or grey scale. These are second heaven dreams that reveal satan's plan, and God is letting us see them so we can pray against them, avert them or stop them from coming to pass or alert others about them. Satan is non-color, but God is full of color. God created color. Color is a good thing and God created

207

us to look good in color and for color to look good to us. Satan is the absence of and opposite of light, but God is light.

Deliverance Dreams: Their purpose is to remove demons and demonic problems in our lives.

Direction Dreams: He gets us to change direction to prevent harm, or to bring us into our destiny. Joseph was warned in a dream to take Jesus to Egypt. (Matthew 2:13) This kind of dream may also have a higher level of revelation or may convey a sense of urgency. They can also show us His desire for us as well.

False Dreams: Dreams that come from satan. *(Jeramiah 29:8 & Zechariah 10:2)*

Fear Dreams: These come from your own fears that you may have had from your own childhood or past. It is not foretelling what is going to come, but because the enemy of fear has come in through legal grounds through things that have happened to you such as un-forgiveness, bitterness, and other legal entries which allow the enemy to attack you. Satan tries to give dreams that will increase your fear and increase his legal right to attack, and pretty soon the thing you fear comes upon you, because you have opened the door of fear to bring more fear. *(Job 3:25)* The principle of Mark 4:24, is that the more we have, more will be added. It doesn't matter if the original fear is unfounded or not, it is still legal ground for the enemy. The answer is to saturate yourself with the truth of God's love which drives out all fear.

Flushing Dreams: Dreams that need to go down the toilet. They shower off slime and dirt from our daily activities. We are in the world but not of the world. We can have issues on us from the world and spirits we have picked up, that need to be cleansed, so God uses dreams to cleanse us before they can become part of us. We can have dreams depicting what others have and have imparted to us, and so the dream is not about us, but it is God washing it off us so it does not become part of us.

A to Z Christian Dream Symbols Dictionary

Healing dreams: They can bring emotional healing and forgiveness, and bring love between people you could not get along with. It can also be a physical healing. You can have a person or angel pray for you in a dream and you were healed, and when you wake up find you were really healed.

Impartation dreams: God uses dreams to download his heart, wisdom, anointing, and secrets to take you to the next level. An angel sometimes may appear to bring this about.

Intrinsic dreams: These deal with heart issues or relationship issues.

Extrinsic Dreams: Focus is on others rather than ourselves such as people groups. nations, cities, churches, etc.

Intercession Dreams: Usually to get us to pray for someone else, but at times for ourselves. Maybe there are problems that are coming your way that through intercession can be adverted.

Invention Dreams: God gives us witty inventions in all areas. He gives us ideas for our benefit and for the benefit of others. Many great inventions, medical cures, songs, etc. have come from dreams.

Prophecy and Revelation Dreams: Things that are happening or are going to happen in the world, your church, your family, your state or city.

Self-Condition Dreams: These tell us where we are with God. God told Ebimmelech that he was a dead man for taking Abraham's wife into his harem. *(Genesis 20:3)*

Soul Dreams: These dreams concern the mind, will, and emotion. We can dream our own opinion about something that has become strong in us. We can have soulish dreams about something we want so badly that we end up dreaming about it and we think it is God, but it is our own soul's desire instead of His desire. (*Jeremiah. 29:8*) We can also cause things to be dreamed by casting away restraint and demanding our own way.

Spiritual Warfare Dreams: These dreams are life threatening events that often come in the form of nightmares. They are attacks against us and others that involve life threatening events. They tell us the enemy hates us and lets us know we must be doing something right. These dreams also tell us we don't have to live in these attacks constantly, but with the power and breath of God and His word, we can destroy these attacks.

Warning Dreams: Dreams that warn us about something that might take place, or warn us so we can change directions to prevent something from happening, or warn us so we can pray against an attack that is coming from the enemy. A dream about an old girl or boy friend may for example may be a warning that you are going back to some old habits, and if you do not change directions, you may not be able to avoid being caught up in an old habit or sin. It is often a warning to not to do certain things.

Word of Knowledge Dreams: These dreams often give solutions to problems in our lives, work, or ministry which are words of knowledge or words of wisdom dreams. He will also give us answers to problems that we need to solve. He often gives me (*John Mark*) messages through dreams.

Interpretation Comes in One of Four Ways

Reveals meaning by an angel like in Daniel. What comes to us in clear revelation also places a much harder demand on us. The greater the revelation, the greater the responsibility.

A to Z Christian Dream Symbols Dictionary

Simultaneously speaking the meaning to us while we are dreaming. We know what the dream is and what it means while it is happening. We hear a voice or simply know what the dream means as it is happening.

By writing it down. Something happens between our eyes, brain and hand as we write, that does not happen in any other way. David had this experience as he was going to build the tabernacle. As he was drawing the plans, he had an open vision. (I Chronicles 28:19) As David wrote it down, the Lord gave him understanding. God told Hosea to write the vision down and make it plain. The Lord gives us understanding as we write our vison down.

He may choose to unfold the meaning of the dream as we mature in our understanding of the ways of God. The glory of God to conceal a matter, but the glory of the king to search the matter out. (Proverbs.25:2) God may hide the meaning of the dream intentionally so we will seek Him and His wisdom out. He knows the intrigue and vacuum will drive us to search Him out and find the answer, and in the process we often will learn more going through the process than in the answer. God is really into process. It is not a sign of immaturity to not know the answers, but it is the glory of the king to search the matter out. Maybe God wants to make us more kingly. We always learn more in the process than in the answer.

Dream interpretation comes out of relationship. Without Him, we cannot remember or interpret our dreams. All interpretation is ultimately from the Lord, therefore, we must develop an intimate relationship with Him so we can hear His voice. Also God loves us to chase Him. If it was easy, we would never chase Him.

Interpretation can come from things around us, and things that are part of our life such as colloquial expressions such as chip off the old block. God will often use things that are familiar with us, and often things that only we would know about, such as things in our past, around the home we grew up in, etc.

Four Levels of Interpretation

Literal: This is the easiest, because God speaks plainly to us, but it also has the greatest responsibility. Greater knowledge always equates to greater responsibility. He will also speak to new and immature believers in this manner.

Allegorical: Which means, "this is that," such as Peter speaking on the day of Pentecost as he referred to Joel's prophecy.

Philosophical: It is about who is in control. When Peter was speaking in Acts 2 about Joel's prophecy he was also speaking of metaphors that stand for other things. When he spoke of old men and young men, he was speaking metaphorically of maturity levels in the faith.

Hidden meaning: Things that are not easily understood such as in Revelation, Daniel and Ezekiel. Many or most dreams are of this nature

Helps to Interpret Dreams

Read and reread Scripture, especially the parables, and passages that use metaphors. This will give us principles and keys to help in understanding our dreams.

Interpretation is a by-product of our relationship with God. We are not guaranteed an interpretation. It is more than just knowing the tools because all revelation only comes by Holy Spirit. God will never remove our need for His precious Holy

A to Z Christian Dream Symbols Dictionary

Spirit. Dreams can come from everyday colloquial expressions and things, such as a chip off the old block, family traits, or nicknames that only you may understand. Genesis 4:8 says interpretation belongs to God. The reality is that Holy Spirit alone can give us the true meaning. Only He can tell if a porpoise means porpoise or purpose, or a c-section can mean c-section or see-section. The most important part of interpretation is the act of asking God for the interpretation. The best way to understand metaphors is to read the Scriptures, especially the parables. The principles for interpreting dreams are the same for parables. If we ever turn it into a formula we will abandon Him and His word. The main principle in interpretation is relationship with Him and His word.

Don't make it complex. Reduce the dream to its simplest form and build on that. If we focus on all the details we will lose the true meaning, like the mustard seed in the parable. We are not to focus on the details of the mustard seed, but focus on the message of that which was small became big. Take the simple and interpret from the context of the dream to get a true meaning. Like a letter from someone, we don't key on the separate words, but the overall message. The individual words simply help to clarify the overall message. Putting too much focus on details will make the interpretation obscure.

Where am I in this dream? Am I bystander watching, or am I taking part in the dream? If an observer, you are a witness because God doesn't do anything without a witness.

Are you just helping? If you are helping or working with other people, then it is probably not about you, but it may impact you because you are part of the group.

Are you the focus? Are you the main character and is everyone watching you? Are you the one that things are happening to?

Make a list of the objects in your dreams. Was there a connection to the objects and you, or connected to what you were trying to do?

Make a list of your emotions. How were you feeling in the dream? Were you happy, sad, angry or fearful? Your emotions will help determine if the dream is positive or negative.

What places or locations occur most often when the dream ends?

Are there other main characters? There may be times when you are the main character, and other times you may play a supporting role. Were the other people faceless, familiar, or strangers?

Are there other objects and other areas that are important to the dream? You will know these things by the intensity of your feelings or thoughts about the dream. You will for example notice a particular car or bold print on a page that seems to be more important. There are things that God will highlight in a dream.

To understand dreams of other people, you need to have God give you their dream vocabulary. What a dog means to you may mean something else to them and will determine the interpretation. To you a dog may mean joy, but to someone else, it may mean fear.

What about this object is like or parallel to you? How are you like this object? Does it remind you about someone's character or actions, or yours?

Is it hard or soft? Is it slick or rough? Is it round or square? Is it long or short? Does it turn or not turn? Is it metal, wood, hollow or solid, crooked or straight? Was it cold or hot? How does it relate to you. Is it being used properly or miss-used? If miss-used, it could for example be saying you are misusing a gift from God. It could be saying you are cold or hot, being soft and comforting, or cold and hard. It could be saying you are full or empty. Steel usually means hard, while wood usually means compassion.

A to Z Christian Dream Symbols Dictionary

Ask Holy Spirit to reveal how the object parallels the attitudes or functions in your life, your field of work or as you as a husband or father.

How do these things help its function and purpose? What ways do the things you have that help you to do the things God has called you to do?

What would hinder the object from being used in the way it was made? How can it be misused? How could you misuse what God has given you? How can what He has given you to do be misused and damage you or others? Hebrews says the exercise of our gift can help us to discern good and evil.

Scenes. Sometimes we may have more than one dream in a night, but often it is the same dream with more than one scene. They are all about one thing, but different facets and perspectives of the same issue.

Multiple Dreams and scenes: It usually is the same dream, but often shows different perspectives.

Context of the dream: Where is the focus? Is it on the person, job, situation, etc.? The person may not really stand for the person. In other words, a person named Fred, may not really stand for Fred, but sometimes the name itself may stand for something. The context will tell you what it means, such as if it is about church, work, family, etc.

Is the person male or female? Does the object have a male or female personality?

Were they a leader such as a president, congressmen, pastor or spiritual leader? If a pastor delivers a message, it could mean you are to be more pastoral. Leaders coming to you means it is a prophetic word to you.

Is this person familiar to you? Are they a stranger to you? If they are familiar or have a familiar feel to them, then it is from the

Lord. If they are not familiar to you and you have an uncomfortable feeling, then it probably not from the Lord, so don't pay attention to what they are telling you in your dream.

Were people or objects aggressive or friendly? What emotions did they provoke in you? How did you feel around them? What emotions did you provoke in them? Angels and Holy Spirit may at times be elevated above you, and are usually faceless.

Negative or positive dream? Is what is happening producing a good or negative feeling?

Ask Holy Spirit to help you remember your dreams. If you are not remembering your dreams, ask Holy spirit why you don't remember them.

Process is personal: Much depends on your background. Does your background produce a God of love, security, fear, etc.? A dog may mean friend to you, but may mean fear and an enemy to someone else.

Ask Holy Spirit to wake you up so you can write it down. Establish a habit of getting up early to help you remember the dream. Discipline yourself to develop the habit. It takes 21 days to establish a habit and after that it becomes easier.

Write it down immediately so you won't forget, including everything that applies to the future and someone else. God always is after a response from us, including in dreams.

To develop short term memory, try to remember all about today and going back to one year ago, such as what you are wearing and doing.

To improve long term memory, try to remember some things you were doing when you were five years old. Remember the house, what it looked like, the cars in your past and what they looked like. Remembering the past will help us remember the

A to Z Christian Dream Symbols Dictionary

dreams we had last night.

Not everyone will be able to interpret your dreams. Your friends know you too well to be objective as they tend to believe the best about you and the worst of others. Learn to go to people with a gift of discernment.

Dreams are not tied to depth as we know it, such as height, space, time, or soul.

Dreams can allow us to transcend our age, we can look any age and even look through someone else's eyes.

****

Other Dream Interpreters Guidelines

Journaling your dreams

Keep track of symbols, feelings, colors, etc. to find patterns and what they normally mean to you.

Ask the Lord what the symbol means for you.

Color code your dreams, colors, symbols, etc. You may even try to diagram your dreams.

If you are artistic, you can do sketches to help interpretation.

Read it over and over out loud to get a better grasp of understanding.

Ask the Lord to give you another dream to help you understand this dream.

Write down symbols in order of your dreams and next to each one, your association or feelings, such as anger, fear, etc.

Ways To Receive Or Help Interpretation

God can instantly reveal a dream or we can receive simultaneous interpretation,

When writing it down, ask questions such as, what was I feeling or what does this mean to me.

It is important to get 8 hours of sleep because the last hour of our sleep cycles will give opportunities for dreams, which we use to process life, especially our emotions.

Dreams can reflect what we already know in our subconscious. It sometimes helps to rehearse or examine our dreams in prayer.

The images and symbols in our dreams awaken in us emotions that need to be processed. God will use emotions in our dreams to deal with issues we are not dealing with when we are awake. Sometimes goofy and random dreams can mean you are not really dealing with issues or taking them serious while awake.

Our heart will often communicate in pictures, therefore characters in dreams often represent parts of ourselves. Dreams often tell us in pictures the struggles we are having in life, and our hearts are trying to communicate a reality in our lives.

Isolate emotions and take them to the Lord for interpretation. What is going on in your life? If a car is going backwards, what part of your life do you feel is going backwards? If you are being chased, how do you feel chased or pressured in life? If naked, do you feel exposed in life? Actions in dreams often reflect our life.

What is the dominant aspect of the person in your dream? It will often represent an aspect about you.

A to Z Christian Dream Symbols Dictionary

Dreams generally concern issues we are presently or will be dealing with. What is going on in your life now or will soon be going on?

The final interpretation must come from be witnessed by heart of the person who has the dream.

Proper interpretation show dreams are to reveal, help, build up, give direction, but never to destroy. God is always good and any dream from Him will always bring peace and never fear or anxiety.

Never make an important life decision based on dream.

Keep a short sin account because sin in your life will hinder you from receiving an accurate interpretation. The exception is when God uses a dream to point out sin so we will repent.

Keep a pad and pen at your bedside and always record your dreams as soon as possible after you receive them. You don't have to write all the small details, but important things like the people involved, any objects or colors that stood out, and you emotions. Don't worry about scribbling ad you can rewrite and fill in the details when you are fully awake.

If you are the main actor, it is always about and for you, but if it then switched to being an observer, it means it is affecting you, but may mostly be for and about others

Even if someone is helping with the interpretation, the symbols in dreams are always personal to the dreamer, therefore the final interpretation always belongs to the dreamer. Even if the helper has a gift in the interpretation of dreams, their interpretation will always have confirmation from the spirit of the dreamer.

The majority of our dreams are about the one who had the dream, however if it is about you combined with being an observer, then pray for guidance in determining who the dream is mainly for, of if God gave it to you so you could intercede for them or possibly intervene in some way.

If for intervention, then pray for God's timing, guidance, and humility in approaching those for whom the dream is given.

No matter your level of experience, you can be sure Holy Spirit will make sure you the proper interpretation. The main key is to not ignore your dream, but to be diligent in pursuing the interpretation.

Recurring dreams or recurring themes means God is trying to bring you an important message for your life. God is the giver and interpreter of your dream, so stay close to Him if you want understanding.

Believe that your dreams are important, therefore give yourself permission to have and remember them.

To increase dream activity try to wake up without an alarm clock because most dreams occur during the last hour of sleep.

About the Author

John Mark Volkots, a former pastor along with his amazing wife Ramona, are itinerant ministers bringing the Father's Heart of love to the nations through teaching/preaching & Father Heart Encounter Schools.

For more information or to schedule meetings, visit healing4thenations.net

Feel free to email at jmvolkots@gmail.com with any questions or thoughts you may have. It would also be greatly appreciated if you would leave a review on Amazon.

Other Books by John Mark Volkots

HOW I DEFEATED CANCER And How You Too Can Defeat Cancer & Terminal Diseases
A major revision of a book originally called, "3 Days to Defeat Cancer." In addition to defeating cancer and other major dis-

eases, it addresses reasons people fail to be healed and how to overcome them, how to position yourself to be healed, how to keep your healing, the role of forgiveness in healing, the difference between authentic and false forgiveness, healing of heart wounds, positive steps to build faith and a godly identity, plus steps to develop intimacy with the Lord. In the Appendix are worksheets and prayers to overcome hindrances to healing, prayers for healing wounds in our hearts, along with other life giving prayers.

WHAT A CRAZY LIFE One man's journey in life, and how stupid, brilliance and a great imagination can live together in one person.
Guaranteed to make you laugh, but more important, you will discover how God takes a person with normal weakness and uses all things good and not so good and works them for good. Hopefully you will also discover the love and favor that God wants to bestow on all of us.

Printed in Great Britain
by Amazon